Story

Story

A Handbook

Jacqueline S. Thursby

Greenwood Folklore Handbooks

GREENWOOD PRESS
Westport, Connecticut • London

Library of Congress Cataloging-in-Publication Data

Thursby, Jacqueline S., 1940–
    Story : a handbook / Jacqueline S. Thursby.
        p. cm.—(Greenwood folklore handbooks, ISSN 1549–733X)
    Includes bibliographical references and index.
    ISBN 0–313–33430–7 (alk. paper)
    1. Folklore—Classification.   2. Folk literature—Themes, motives.   3. Folklore—
History and criticism.   4. Folklore—Authorship. I.   Title. II.   Series.
    GR74.6.T48   2006
    398.012—dc22   2005037901

British Library Cataloguing in Publication Data is available.

Library of Congress Catalog Card Number: 2005037901
ISBN: 0–313–33430–7
ISSN: 1549–733X

First published in 2006

Greenwood Press, 88 Post Road West, Westport, CT 06881
An imprint of Greenwood Publishing Group, Inc.
www.greenwood.com

Printed in the United States of America

The paper used in this book complies with the
Permanent Paper Standard issued by the National
Information Standards Organization (Z39.48-1984).

10   9   8   7   6   5   4   3   2   1

Copyright Acknowledgments

The author and publisher gratefully acknowledge permission to reprint the following material:

Excerpts from Lori Langer de Ramirez, short version of La Fontaine's "The Crow and the Fox" (Miscositas.com, 2005). Reprinted with permission.

Excerpts from Margaret Fleming, "Gilgamesh" (pp. 15–16) and "The Ramayana," *Teaching the Epic* (Urbana: NCTE, 1974). Copyright © 2006 by the National Council of Teachers of English. Reprinted with permission.

Excerpts from *Metamorphoses* by Ovid, translated by Charles Martin. Copyright © 2004 by Charles Martin. Used by permission of W. W. Norton & Company, Inc. This selection may not be reproduced, stored in a retrieval system, or transmitted in any form or by any means without the prior written permission of the publisher.

Every reasonable effort has been made to trace the owners of copyrighted materials in this book, but in some instances this has proven impossible. The author and publisher will be glad to receive information leading to more complete acknowledgments in subsequent printings of the book and in the meantime extend their apologies for any omissions.

Contents

Preface

Human beings have expressive minds, and inventing and interpreting information by way of narration and story is basic to everyday life. Mark Turner, in *The Literary Mind,* suggests that "the understanding of a complex of objects, events, and actors [is] organized by our knowledge of *story*" (1996: 5). Who told the first story, and where did it come from? What kind of a story was it? Was it a creation story that told how the earth and sky and people came to be, or was it an action story that described how some animal or fish escaped from hungry hunters? Stories have emerged from every culture that has inhabited the earth. Cave paintings from prehistoric times represent stories or narratives humans have long forgotten. "Currently, we know of the existence of more than 200 caves in Europe containing Paleolithic paintings. Most of the images date from the Magdalenian cultural period, which lasted from 15,000 to 10,000 B.C.E., and 90 per cent of them can be found in France and Spain" (Roberts 1998: 49).

Over time many guesses and explanations have been made, shared, and then discarded about what those ancient figures may have meant. Though we may never know the answers to questions concerning such ancient representations, there is much we do know about stories in general. With each telling, stories weave an individual pattern of meaning according to the intent of the teller and the understanding of the listener. There are many kinds of stories used for many purposes, and this handbook will help you understand more clearly what they are and how they are used.

This handbook focuses on the meaning and use of many different kinds of stories. It is a guide to the world of organized words and ideas that surrounds us, and it will help put into order those words and ideas by presenting narratives both old and new, familiar and unfamiliar, supernatural and real, from faraway places and from your own neighborhood and family. It is nearly impossible to imagine a world without stories. They shape us into the people we are. They determine our culture, give us information, teach us useful skills, help us to form opinions, and provide a way to express our thoughts. The cave paintings from prehistoric times certainly have stories or narratives associated with them. Perhaps the painted animals and figures were part of hunting or fertility rituals, but we can only guess generally at what they may have meant. When human beings learned to write and keep records, some of their narratives unraveled the mysteries of earlier times. Those early records and stories also created baffling new mysteries that have been wondered about diachronically (through time) even to the present.

There are complex story or narrative ownership discussions between and among folklorists, storytellers, and writers of written literary tales. Ethical questions arise about whose property is whose and how the stories can be used. Among folklorists, the transmission of oral or vernacular stories is simply a way of transmitting information about cultural boundaries, traditions, and the maintenance of the mores and folkways of a group. Exclusive ownership issues concerning stories are not much of an issue because folklorists understand that boundaries can be negotiated, and the whole of society benefits by learning from one another through cultural narratives and artifacts.

Among some village or professional storytellers, there is often great reluctance to tell one another's stories. This is not always true, but in some areas of the world, stories are traditionally passed on through inheritance or permission. On the other hand, there are many storytellers who freely borrow stories from one another and generously encourage others to use their stories and styles. Another group, literary artists, own their stories legally by formal copyright. Though the themes or motifs are often borrowed, the creative work itself is rightfully protected, and wisdom dictates that permission be granted before borrowing too freely from a professional writer's work. The stories you will find described and discussed in this text fall in all of the categories listed above, and more. Additionally, however, stories of experiences and hearsay are often passed along casually without thought of origin or ownership. Narrative exchange is reflective of human nature, and that is how we each participate in shaping the ideas in our world.

Traditional storytelling, or a narrated performance by one person, is an ancient practice for transmitting a variety of information. In the old world, stories were carried from place to place by sailors, merchants, and other travelers. The stories were used to transmit cultural tradition, and they were learned from one generation to the next. Storytelling is used today for that reason, but stories are now used in both entertainment and teaching, and simply for close, social interaction. Stories are used and told by parents, teachers (both religious and secular), and scholars (in every discipline), professional and nonprofessional entertainers, friends, and the unfamiliar woman or man sitting next to you on an airplane or bus. People tell jokes, personal anecdotes, urban myths and legends, and gossip to one another as a part of ordinary daily interaction, and our cultural and social views are strongly influenced by these experiences.

Professional storytellers, or "tellers" as they are often called, have enjoyed a revival of their craft in the last quarter of the twentieth century. Nontraditional storytelling, folklorist and professional storyteller Ruth Stotter states, "may appropriate stories found in published texts, from cultures with which neither the teller nor the audience have firsthand experience. Performance oriented, story interpretation is shaped by the individual teller's personal taste." In the late 1800s, librarians were trained to become storytellers, and "'Story hours' were offered in the U.S. libraries as early as 1896, and in 1909 the American Library Association sponsored a story-hour symposium" (Stotter 1996: 690).

Both the National Association for the Preservation and Perpetuation of Storytelling (NAPPS), founded by Jimmy Neil Smith in 1973, and the Black Storytelling Festival, a yearly event that began in 1983, have promoted storytelling and provided venues for vast U.S. audiences. At the time of this writing, there are more than 1,000 professional storytellers in the United States who perform in "schools, libraries, museums, coffeehouses, theaters, and festivals" (Stotter 1996: 690). There is no clear demarcation between traditional and nontraditional storytelling because both transmit cultural mores and traditions, both inform and entertain, and both establish an intimacy between the teller and the hearer(s).

This text will provide high school students, undergraduates, and general readers with information that explains the some of the story of stories, their elements, and the tellers who share them. The first chapter, an introduction, provides a general history of the topic and its significance. Thousands of years ago, when the complexity of writing as a method of communication and record keeping was just beginning to take shape, most people did not communicate by written forms, but oral or spoken stories flourished even then. They were transmitted from person to person and country to country by word-of-mouth. Stories of creation, mystic rites, angry gods, vision quests, and magic occurrences were found in every culture. Scribes, priests, nobility, and royalty were the elite (upper) segment of various populations, and they used their knowledge of reading and writing as a medium of power. "Writing was quickly recognized as a powerful skill, and through the ranks of [early] Mesopotamian society rose the scribe. . . . With all the power that lay in their hands, the Mesopotamian scribes were an aristocratic elite" (Manguel 1996: 180). There was little effort to teach the broad population to read and write until after the medieval period (500 C.E.–1400 C.E.). Various religions, or belief systems, emerged throughout the world and people constructed stories to answer questions about the birth of the earth, natural phenomena, and the purpose of life. Over time and generations, as these stories were told and repeated, they began to include stories about heros, and families, and events. Out of those stories came myths, legends, folktales, and other kinds of narratives that we read, share, and reinvent even in our own, modern-day society.

Chapter 2 defines and classifies the most significant types of stories, both short and long, and techniques mythologists, folklorists, and storytellers sometimes use. It also discusses how some of the stories have been created. This chapter answers some questions and raises others. Many people seem to think that folklore is *only* storytelling, the retelling of legends and old tales, but that is only *part* of what folklore is. Many stories are called folktales, meaning that the stories have been transmitted from person to person over time by word-of-mouth, but the elements of *folklore* often make up the motifs that appear in many kinds of folktale narrative.

Jokes, riddles, limericks, proverbs, ballads, myth, legends, fairy tales, folktales, mythologies, and other oral lore are classified as oral folklore, and they contain folkloric elements; that is, elements that are familiar in everyday life and are used over and over again. Ethnic stereotypes and slurs, common superstitions such as touching wood for luck, wishes and curses—these are some *elements* or *motifs* of folklore, and there are many, many more. Folklore, then, as repeated practices that pass from person to person, is a constant presence in stories.

In the essay "Documenting Folklore," folklorist William A. Wilson suggested three categories for the study of folklore: things people say (jokes, riddles, proverbs); things people make (rugs, pottery, baskets); and things people do (holiday customs, family traditions, folk dances) (1986: 225). Another important category is things people believe (superstitions, home-cures, folk beliefs, and religions). These elements are present in stories and lived human experience whether it is past or present, foreign or domestic, comedy or tragedy. Many scholars of folktale and stories have written varied classification systems in order to study folktale and stories in a systematic way. This chapter describes some of these systems and explains how to use them for research in both traditional and nontraditional storytelling.

Chapter 3 is made up of story examples and narratives from around the world. Roughly half of the stories in this chapter are from the English-speaking world, and half are from the non-English-speaking world. Story examples will be either traditionally *literary* (or written) or *vernacular* (by word-of-mouth), and the text will identify some of the folklore elements used in both kinds of stories as defined and described in chapter 2.

The discussion will explain why the stories included have lasted over time. Many stories are cast aside because they simply no longer have meaning to people in their present life setting. Maybe they are from another time that is unfamiliar to the hearer (or reader), or maybe the story simply didn't serve any purpose. For a good story to be considered great and lasting, it must appeal to the human condition. That is, the reader must find something of herself or himself in it, or at least they must find someone or something they recognize and to which they can relate.

Human beings, across time and space, share many biological, emotional, and cultural commonalities. Everyone experiences hunger, fatigue, happiness, sadness, anger, gratitude, envy, pride, or humility at one time or another. People generally like to be noticed and validated, and people hope for physical and emotional safety and continuity of what is familiar to them. Peace of mind is a quest the human family seeks, and stories that last usually appeal to these and other universal biological and emotional human needs. The human conditions listed here are mostly biological or emotional responses to life, but there is another huge and very influential category of the human condition, namely cultural. Human beings construct ideas in an attempt to somehow put their worlds in order. Called cultural or social constructions, people make up guidelines, rules, formal and informal laws, folkways, and mores, in order to structure their families, communities, and even nations. The main way these constructions are transferred from one generation to the next, through home life, schools, churches, and community practice, is through shaping stories, and, along with various stories, some of this is discussed in the third chapter.

The fourth chapter discusses scholarship and approaches that have been practiced over time to try to explain the structure and meaning of stories. Questions about stories have been posed since the time of Aristotle (384–322 B.C.E.), and perhaps before. What is a story? How do stories work? What helps us to remember them? What are the elements of a good story? What parts must it have to hold the reader's interest? Many classifications and approaches have attempted to explain the fundamental meaning of stories and why we continue to use them. From tale-typing to lists of elements and functions to ever-changing literary criticism to folkloric approaches to narratology (a close examination of the acts and elements of narration), scholars continue to make informed guesses about how stories continue to both entertain us and shape our cultural and social behaviors. Certainly questioning is fundamental to the human condition. Humans are curious about their environment, their past, and their future. They wonder about their survival. Stories, shared one to another, help to dispel confusion. They can teach old principles in new ways, increase our ability to think and analyze, and weigh pros and cons before drawing conclusions. It is through stories that we learn about other people and other cultures, and we learn from their ancient wisdom. Stories deepen our understanding. Theories and discoveries about how stories work have emerged from many sources, and it is interesting to look at some of the more popular speculations.

Chapter 5 discusses the contexts in which story or narrative is used. The application of stories is vast. Artists around the world, over time and space, have interpreted and reinterpreted stories in poetry, prose, music, films, painting, sculpture, comics, and now even in digital form. Stories are used in advertising, and there is commodification (marketing or selling) of popular story motifs or symbols. For instance, from themed Halloween costumes to tableware, retailers make available to buyers goods that represent characters from Ulysses to Luke Skywalker, Cinderella to the three little pigs, Noah and the ark to Disney's Little Mermaid (and so much more). Youngsters around the world wear Harry Potter glasses. This contextual chapter discusses the impact of story and narrative on the contemporary culture in which we are living.

This volume supplies a glossary and index to aid readers in understanding and navigating the text. It also includes a bibliography and list of web resources to lead readers to further research.

WORKS CITED

Manguel, Alberto. 1996. *A History of Reading.* New York: Penguin Putnam.

Roberts, J. M. 1998. *Prehistory and the First Civilizations.* Vol. 1 *of The Illustrated History of the World.* London: Time Life/Duncan Baird.

Stotter, Ruth. 1996. "Storytelling." In *American Folklore: An Encyclopedia,* ed. Jan Brunvand, 690–91. New York: Garland.

Turner, Mark. 1996. *The Literary Mind.* New York: Oxford University Press.

Wilson, William A. 1986. "Documenting Folklore." In *Folk Groups and Folklore Genres: An Introduction,* ed. Elliott Oring, 225–54. Logan: Utah State University Press.

One

Introduction

Questioning is fundamental to the existence of human beings, and stories satisfy many of those questions, though the answers stories give may not be satisfying to all listeners. Humans are endowed with inquiring minds that lead them to find the means to satisfy complex and innate needs and goals. We seek and even construct explanations to clear away confusions. In antiquity our curiosity led us to probe into neighboring caves and jungles, and in our own day we explore other countries and even other galaxies and planets. Inquiry strengthens our own ability to analyze and deduce answers, and through inquiry we also learn about other people and establish new relationships.

Folklorists gather, classify, analyze, and discuss information. The folkloric method is one of many ways to pursue lines of inquiry about the world we live in and the people with whom we associate. We question, and we encourage others to question. Question this text as you read. I suggest that you ask yourself how to apply some of the strategies for discerning meaning that you will find here. Many students of folklore find that when they learn to analyze informal human behavior, they see the life around them in a much different and often more respectful light. Cultural studies such as folklore help us understand the expressive behavior of humankind, and much of that behavior is represented by the peoples' stories.

In a simple sense, sometimes called "reductive" by scholars, components of human existence are things either biological or cultural. Though we as humans try to control genetics and the chemical makeup of our bodies, even our weight, biological cause-and-effect principles of nature remain in control. Culture, on the other hand, is constructed and reconstructed through human ingenuity and imagination. A scholar named Alexander Eliot wrote that as the atmosphere bathes and serves as a life-shield to the earth and keeps it stable and healthy, the "mythosphere," or imaginative domain of stories, keeps the human mind healthy. It is in the story-domain of our minds that we construct worldviews that shape our lives (Eliot 1990: 1). We are socialized as we grow up, usually by our elders, and then at some point most of us reexamine what we have been taught. Over time we reevaluate our lives from more experienced perspectives and then adjust and carry on in life realizing that our vast combinations of understandings need reshaping every now and then. Stories help us do that. There are many experiences and nuggets of wisdom that we learn from stories rather than firsthand experience.

Since the dawn of time, human beings have tried to define themselves through their expressed culture; that is, repetitive traditions. Those traditions, often expressed through stories, material artifacts, or behavior, were named *folklore*, a term coined in England by a nineteenth-century scholar named William J. Thoms. He wanted an Anglo-Saxon word to replace the Latin-based term *popular antiquities*. Modern folklorists use the term to designate cultural items that are passed on by vernacular (oral) or customary tradition. It is important to remember that folklore can emerge from any culture of any social, economic, or ethnic level. The word *folk* does not refer to the less educated or less financially secure.

From starting a fire to avoiding it, from making or finding early water vessels to tanning hides, vernacular transmission of traditional ways of living, called folklore, has carried humanity from generation to generation. There isn't a lot we can do to change or control biology, but our ability and inclination to construct and reconstruct cultural perceptions, controls, and worldview is almost infinite. We describe and transmit most of these constructions through verbal exchange; that is, through myth, legend, folktales, anecdotes, ballads, jokes, proverbs, limericks, rhymes, and esoteric (known to an in-group) storylike general conversation.

How do the most familiar stories, in this case, folk and fairy tales, begin? There are countless ways, of course, but people in the Western or Occidental world often carry an expected stereotype associated with story beginnings. Even so, there are many ways of beginning, and the following quotation lists just a few. Sometimes the beginning phrase suggests what is to come after.

Many folktales open with standard beginnings that capture the attention of the listener and establish time and mood. Sometimes these beginning phrases vary in folktales from different cultures. "Once upon a time" is a recognizable opening for many English variants, while folktales from the Philippines open with

"In the first times," and many African storytellers begin with "A story, a story, let it come, let it go." These phrases not only help to place the listener in a "dream world where anything is possible" (Sutherland 1997) but also provide a hint at the culture the story may reflect. (Roe, Alfred, and Smith 1998: 169)

Though Americans often seem to think of stories as formal narratives that begin with "once upon a time" and end with "and they lived happily ever after," that occurs only in one genre (classification) of story type. This discussion will help you recognize and use many other types of oral accounts that can be called story. Reflect on yesterday for a few minutes. Can you remember any stories that you may have been told? Think about conversations that may have taken place before school or work, between classes or tasks, or even in class or at the proverbial water cooler. Did you get a note from anyone? Did someone pass along some interesting (or disturbing) gossip? Or, did you hear a new joke? Maybe you watched television before you left home. The commercials seen on television today are usually presented in narrative or story form. Some of the advertising is so captivating that you may have even remarked that some of the commercials are better than the programs they interrupt or the products they represent. Think about the yearly Super Bowl and its sponsors. Those commercials do a great storytelling job. In their efforts to try to persuade us to use their products, they usually use verbal or material motifs that are familiar to us. They try to grab our attention and keep it with a mini-story that has a beginning, a middle, and an end. The underlying concept is often an appeal to our improved happiness if we buy and use their products. Several advertisements declare on television and in magazines, for instance, that you will be much more popular if you use their mouthwash, drink their soda, or drive their high-powered car.

When we hear and then pass stories along, any kind of stories, they enter the realm of what folklorists simply call folklore, or the lore of the folk (meaning all of us). Though many of the world's stories or narratives have been written down, it has been suggested that when they are passed orally through several tellers and listeners, the stories become a part of expressive human culture and are considered to be folklore. The many kinds of folk narrative, from fairy tales to gossip, help to determine who we are and what we value.

Stories that are invented or created by talented writers or journalists are literary works. Though they may use folkloric items in the development of their stories, their creations did not really emerge from the lived culture of people. There is a difference between the authenticity of a tall tale about a mythic Paul Bunyan or Pecos Bill and a shared story about actual lumberjack initiations in the deep woods of Oregon or Michigan. This point will be discussed later in the text; it is an important concept because it points to different kinds of stories and varied uses. Think about a smooth, polished stone, and in your mind compare it to a seashell covered with oddly shaped barnacles and bumps. The smooth stone represents a writer's literary creation—an invented and polished literary narrative. Many oral tales have been passed through that process, and where they were once invented and rarely told exactly the same way twice, they were polished, written, and became static. The rough shell represents traditional, vernacular folklore. In its transmission, it has been tossed about, added to, broken and chipped here and there, and has emerged as a sturdy survivor. The ancient Nordic stories of Odin and Thor are good examples of those wonderful, complex, added upon, barnacled stories.

Story, as a word, emerges from the ancient Latin word *historia*. That word evolved into the Old French word *estoire* and entered Middle English as *storie*. Our word *story* was derived from the Middle English. According to one dictionary I consulted, "story, the broadest in scope of these words, refers to a series of connected events, true or fictitious, that is written or told with the intention of entertaining or informing" (Agnes 2002: 1413). The attribute that qualifies a story for the label of *folklore* is oral repetition. If the story has been casually repeated many times in oral tradition, and even recorded or written down at some point, then it can be called folklore. For many years, stories or narrative were only considered folklore if they were vernacular, or oral, and not written down. With the creation of archives and libraries in many universities around the world, and an increase in the number of people gathering these stories, many have been written, published, and then filed away in various archives. Because of that, *folklore* as a term has different implications than it had years ago. Though there are many definitions, it is expressive culture created and repeated by human beings and reflective of their lived culture. As stated above, the "folk" can be of any culture or socio-economic class from doctors and lawyers to ranchers/farmers and blue-collar laborers, male or female, adult or child, in any country of the world. True folklore is not a literary invention by a professional writer. It emerges from people's lived experience, and if it is repeated and passed along, it is valid whether or not it is written.

To explain more fully the relationship between folklore and story, understand that items identified as folkloric appear in all kinds of stories that are not classified as folktales or fairy tales. From the material lore of an apron of fig leaves representing what Adam and Eve covered themselves with in the Garden of Eden as used in the high Masonic rituals, to the magic wand in *Harry Potter*, and from the oral lore of superstitions in *Huckleberry Finn* to the customary and stereotypical pirate behaviors in Gore Verbinski's *Pirates of the Caribbean: The Curse of the Black Pearl,* literary writers have used, both consciously and unconsciously, elements of traditional folklore to shape their stories.

Looking for folkloric elements in stories helps the reader to connect more fully with meaning. One of the ultimate purposes of stories is to create *empathy,* or understanding for others through shared information. By listening to and reading stories from our own and other cultures, we discover that though people have constructed different languages and life systems, our biological needs and emotional responses have been much the same throughout time.

Adam and Eve leaving the garden covered with skins in place of the fig leaf aprons.

Stories help us understand one another, and when we understand, we have better relationships.

ORAL TRADITIONS, NARRATIVES, AND RITUALS

How did the world come to be? We see galaxies of light, the sun, the moon, the mountains, and oceans, and like primitive humankind, we wonder. In our modern age, we have discovered many scientific explanations, but long ago humans constructed creation stories to provide some kind of answers to those mysteries. Did the earth and humans hatch from an egg as the ancient Greeks and Romans, and many Asian cultures, seemed to believe? Was it created in six days by a great, powerful god, as it is explained in the Hebrew testaments? Or did the earth reside on the back of a turtle with people and animals climbing to the surface from deep within the world sphere as some of the North American Indian myths suggest? Sometimes these old creation stories are incorporated into the peoples' religion or belief systems, rituals, and practices; other times they have been perceived as having secular (non-religious) purposes. The many examples of different kinds of stories presented in chapter 3 will help to inform you as you explore the fascinating and often interconnected web of world narratives.

Mystic rites and rituals, from birth to death, honor and celebrate significant transitions or rites-of-passage through life. In the ancient Greek tradition, the Eleusinian Mysteries initiated, with deepest reverence, both men and women of all ages into the symbolic meanings of life as the ancient Greeks understood it. With processions, baptisms, seals and symbols (passwords), the initiates were guided by a hierophant (a holy teacher) through various symbolic lesser and greater mysteries and rituals similar to Egyptian rites of Isis. After nine days, the initiates were considered to have been informed about the origins and ends of life (Taylor 1980: xii).

Religious rituals include christening, blessing, or naming ceremonies for infants. A folk belief attached to the christening of babies in the Episcopal or Anglican Church suggests that if the little one cries during the ceremony, it will have a holy and protected life because all of the evil spirits that surround it will be frightened away by the shrill cries. At the other end of life, there are folk beliefs, rituals, and stories to help maintain both dignity and peace of mind for the living and the dying. In the Muslim tradition, honey or tiny sips of cool water are sometimes given to the dying in their last moments. It is believed that the spirit leaves the body through the throat. The honey keeps the spirit sweet, and the water makes the spirit's journey easier. It is believed that, soon after death, the deceased will be questioned by the angels Munkar

Early Egyptian rites of Isis
influenced later rituals in
the Mediterranean region.

and Nakír, and the deceased's salvation depends on correct and complete answers (Kassis 1997: 54). The dying are coached with the correct answers, kept comfortable, and hopefully kept sweet enough that they will not cry out against their god in their anguish. No believer would deliberately incur god's wrath.

Stories about angry gods abound in world mythologies. This might have something do to with instilling fear in people in order to keep social order, but one of the most interesting of these angry gods is Odin. He is also known by the names of Wotan and Woden, All father (*Alfodr*), Father of the Slain (*Valfodr*), and many more. One early writer, Snorri Sturluson (c.1220), listed 49 or more names that reflected elements of Odin's fierce character (Auerbach 1997: 28). Sturluson himself was a source of interest and stories. He was a very different Icelandic landowner and chieftan, well traveled and well educated. In 1218 "he visited the Norwegian court, where he was granted feudal titles. Snorri was a poet . . . and so composed his *Prose Edda*, which is at the same time a handbook on the rules of style and metre and a manual on Scandinavian mythology" (Simpson 1997:17). One of the reasons Sturluson, a Christian, wrote the epic tales of the Scandinavian

Odin, sometimes called Wotan or Woden, "All Father" or "Father of the Slain."

tradition was that he recognized that they would be lost if not recorded. Though other early writers recorded tales also, Sturluson created the most easily understood collection.

Odin was the primary god of the Northern European Norse and Germanic tribes. Odin had one eye and wore a dark, wide-brimmed hat that cast a mysterious shadow over his face. He roamed widely, was unpredictable, and could turn against favorites without notice; further, it was said that unpredictably he would award rather than punish the unjust. Hanging, stabbing, and burning are ritual practices associated with Odin, and in the ancient Nordic poem *Havamal* ("Words of the High One"), the story is told of how Odin hung

Thor, a well-known and powerful Scandinavian god. He usually wielded a hammer.

from the world tree (Yggdrasill) for nine days without food or water after having been slashed with a spear. The story carries some Christian elements, but it is difficult to determine consistent relationships between the two.

Thor was another very well known and powerful god in the ancient world of the Scandinavians; although he was called the god of thunder, his character was helpful and benign. Odin was the god of the aristocracy, while Thor was much loved by farmers and laborers, who made up the majority of these early civilizations. Both of these great Nordic gods traveled far and near in pursuit of giants, their sworn enemies. Giants, a noun used as a metaphor (a word that symbolizes meaning beyond its literal use), can mean any manner of things. A metaphorical giant can be anything that portends evil—from violence to deception. In these early days of the world, and in many cultures up to the present, individuals have sought protection from the evils, or "giants," of the world. Stories, with various characters and motifs, emerge that describe these challenges.

In many of the Native American traditions, young people embark on a rite-of-passage called a vision quest to find their totem animal and personal attributes and identity. It is believed that knowing these things will help guard them from their own weaknesses and from the evil intentions of others, including supernatural forces of evil. In metaphorical terms, we might call these fears "giants," not unlike the ancient people of the North. Wallace Black Elk, a Lakota Sioux, explained that isolation is an important part of the vision quest, and over time, personal visions and ritual responses lead the questers to higher levels of understanding. The vision quest, Black Elk tells us, is initially four days long, and the individual has to go through four stages of understanding. Even so, the process may need to be repeated many times with diligent prayer, hard work, and again, complete isolation before real understanding begins to happen (Black Elk 1990: 43).

Questions about the universe and natural phenomena began this section. Scientists have theorized and attempted to answer these questions, but there is still much that remains unknown. Hearing great thunder and feeling the earth shake under one's feet is frightening to most people, and humans from the earliest times have wanted to gain power over the great, destructive forces of nature. As we witnessed in 2004, the great Asian tsunami demonstrated that we have not achieved that control, but there are many who like to think they have. There are also many theories about whether myth or ritual came first, but inherent or present in both, at least anciently and still in some traditions of the world, is *magic*. And just what is magic? Is it weeds and toads, warts and snails, all mixed in a caldron of steaming brew and waved over with a magic wand and then used for casting spells?

Perhaps a better question to ask is: *Why* is magic? From the ancient, priestly Druids in the Celtic tradition, to the shaman, or medicine men, in tribal traditions of both the past and present, there have been powerful leaders who seemed to understand nature enough to have some control over it. Usually powerful and persuasive personalities, they perhaps knew some natural laws and used them, or it could be that they were simply skilled in deceiving their followers. Either way, magic is the practice of using spells, charms, and rituals in seeking or pretending to have power or governance over natural or supernatural forces. Basically, again, reductively, magical behavior can be divided into two huge categories. *Magic,* as a word, is a general term that applies to effective power over the natural or supernatural; *sorcery* implies spells or charms cast over people or places usually for evil or harmful purposes. Magic and sorcery appeal to humans because they suggest mysterious power over any circumstance, including death. There are stories and traditions concerning the pursuit of eternal life, or at least the pursuit of extended youth and long-lasting mortality, and many of these have become classics, such as the Greco-Roman story of Eos and Tithonus (a matter of aging because of the failure to ask a god for youth) and *Faust,* by Goethe (briefly, a story of bargaining with Satan for extra years in order to enjoy power, knowledge, and earthly pleasure).

Folkloric elements and motifs play symbolic roles in these stories and accounts of individuals who have sought to confirm their own eternal survival. In the ancient Sumerian story of *Gilgamesh,* the Oceanic tradition of Maui, the medieval traditions of the early alchemists, and the traditional stories of the Eastern European vampires, we are reminded of the extraordinary effort humans will put forth to overcome the unknown veil of death.

QUESTS FOR IMMORTALITY

The oldest known written and preserved epic in the world may be the Sumerian story of the hero Gilgamesh (Thury and Devinney 2005: 143). Seeking answers about immortality, Gilgamesh wandered through crushing darkness hoping to receive answers from the great sun god, Shamash. The 4,000-year-old narrative reveals, once again, humankind's constant quest for explanations of the human condition; it also reveals a heroic pattern that occurs over and over in stories of heroes and saviors. The hero is somehow called to adventure, crosses a threshold into the unknown, receives supernatural aid, usually meets with a goddess, suffers some kind of atonement, passes through a road of trials, and then returns to his or her people. Symbols of light and darkness, certain common artifacts, and beliefs in the lore of eternal

Gilgamesh wrestling with the Bull of Heaven.

glory once more demonstrate the driving power of constructed explanations in expressive culture. We will see in the next chapter how folklorists have identified and analyzed complex and multiepisodic stories like *Gilgamesh*.

Gilgamesh had been devastated by the death of his best friend, Enkidu, and sought comfort through knowledge. The *Gilgamesh* account in the third chapter of this text will unfold this multilayered plot, which, as is common in many lasting narratives, includes stories framed within one another. Gilgamesh eventually does learn the secret of eternal youth, but a serpent steals it from him. He then, in typical heroic mode, returns to his people where he (or his scribes) engraved the entire adventure story on a stone. Most, though not all, of the tablets upon which the story is written in cuneiform have been found, along with some ancient but later versions, and several versions of the story have been pieced together.

Another ancient quest-for-immortality story tells about the trickster figure, Maui (Maui-tiki-tiki-a-Taranga). From New Zealand to Hawaii, many children are told of the exploits of this founding god. In epic segments, his story includes metaphorical or representational elements. He made a weapon from his grandmother's jawbone. The weapon, like words, was very powerful. Scholars wonder if the jawbone motif itself represented the power of talking. One of the things he did with the jawbone was to cripple the sun so that it would move more slowly across the sky, therefore providing humans with a longer day. It is said that he furnished the world with New Zealand by fishing it up from the bottom of the sea using the jawbone for a hook. He also made fire available to individual humans rather than their always having to get fire from a communal center, and though he quested for immortality, he lost his own life in the process of the quest (Eliot 1990: 81).

Alchemy is an early form of chemistry, and its chief purpose was twofold. First, it was a search for turning base (ordinary) metals into valuable gold, and second, it was a quest to discover the key to perpetual youth. The practice of alchemy had attached to it superstition, mysterious philosophies, and magic. One of the most legendary alchemists was Nicholas Flamel. Historical memory of Flamel has been revived by the appearance of his name in the Harry Potter series by J. K. Rowling. Because of the curious nature of Flamel's work and claims, there are many stories about him.

Questions remain about just what happened to him, and some people wonder if perhaps he was able to discover the secret of immortality and failed to die. He drew many strange illustrations, and in those drawings are folkloric elements related to alchemy and the occult. Triangles, crowns, angels, devils, pestles and mortars, the caduceus (winged medical symbol), and various unusual animals and human beings appear in various positions and relationships in the pictures. Curiosity got the best of some people, and so eventually his grave was opened and his coffin examined. It was empty. The stories of Nicholas Flamel and his wife, Perenelle, are complex and interesting, and they have appeared in literature and oral lore many times since the thirteenth century when they lived. In chapter 3, I will share some of their quest and mention a few other alchemists whose names you might recognize, but you may be left with more unresolved questions than answers!

Though there are many historical characters and groups who have sought the secrets of eternal life over time and in various places around the world, a particularly interesting category of these seekers are the so-called vampires. Well-known

The Alchemist.

The alchemist observing his experiment of possibilities. *The Granger Collection, New York.*

myths, legends, and folktales abound about these mysterious creatures, and those stories have been formed and reformed into televisions shows like *Buffy the Vampire Slayer,* vampire novels by Anne Rice, the new Elizabeth Kostova book, *The Historian,* and several films including Francis Ford Coppola's *Bram Stoker's Dracula* (1992) and Hiroyuki Kitakubo's *Blood: The Last Vampire* (2000).

Vladimir Tepes (1431–76), a ruler in early Romania, is thought to be the source of the Dracula legend. He was a cruel person who destroyed his enemies by impaling them with wooden stakes. For that reason, he was called Vlad the Impaler. Most of the stories of vampires seem to emerge from Eastern Europe, though there are stories of vampires from the Western hemisphere as well. When examining horror stories like these, it is reasonable to ask why we humans enjoy them. Do we like to be shocked? Do we really believe such things? Could there really be such distortions of human life that some could survive indefinitely on others' blood? In the animal world vampire bats (*Desmodus rotundus*) exist in Central and South America, but they do not attack humans. Personally I don't think human vampires exist, but the stories are gruesomely interesting and somewhat worth pondering.

RELIGIONS AND BELIEF SYSTEMS

In today's world, there are countless religions and belief systems, but the five largest of all of the world religions are Judaism, Islam, Christianity, Hinduism, and Buddhism. There are many subsets of each of these, and even combinations of beliefs (syncretism) where the religions have crossed over and adapted ideas from one another. Underlying all of the great religious systems of the world are codes of ethical behavior. In order to teach these behavioral guidelines to adherents, all the major religions use stories in a didactic (teaching) sense. Some of the greatest folklore of the world has emerged from these simple stories, parables, and proverbs invented to teach people how to get along with one another and how to make the best human beings out of themselves. Chapter 3 presents some of these stories; for now, the following brief overview of these five main religions and some of their dominant beliefs will help you further understand the stories you will read later.

Judaism

The religion of the Jews is monotheistic, meaning that central to their religion is a belief in one God. That God, they believe, created the world and led the Jews out of Egyptian bondage. The Hebrew Bible, which has one story after another, is the primary sacred text of Judaism, and the family is the basic unit of Jewish ritual. In the early Judaic tradition, storytelling for entertainment was not acceptable, and the stories told had to represent the orthodox versions approved by the leaders and written in their official scrolls. Even so, the folklore scholar Alan Dundes, reminding us that the oral tradition (folklore) preceded the written, asks: "[I]f the Bible was once folklore, why is it not still folklore? Just because it was written down does not automatically negate its original folkloristic nature" (Dundes 1999: 9). There are, even in the written text, a few examples of storytelling. For instance, in Judges 9:7–20, Jotham narrates a convincing parable to the people of Shechem describing metaphorically the horrible deeds done by their ruler, Abimelech. There are other examples of cursings, deceit, and resolution used to teach these ancient people (Deuteronomy 11:29 and Joshua 9:7).

Most of today's Jews are descended from either Central or Eastern European Jews (Ashkenazim) or Spanish and Portuguese Jews before they were expelled from Spain and Portugal in 1492 (Sephardim). There are currently over 14 million Jews in the world. Primary religious branches among contemporary Jews are Orthodox Judaism, Reform Judaism, and Conservative Judaism. Orthodox Judaism seeks to preserve ancient traditions, Reform Judaism tries to interpret the religion in consideration of modern scholarship and knowledge, and Conservative Judaism attempts to modify orthodox traditions by emphasizing only positive historical elements (Goring and Whaling 1994: 270, 271). The formal Sabbath, for most Jews, continues to be from sundown on Friday to sundown on Saturday.

The Hasidic Jews, whose men generally wear black clothing and also distinctive earlocks of hair, live in communities throughout the world including large settlements in the United States. Each group is led by a rebbe, a Hasidic rabbi. The Hasids trace their heritage as a group to eighteenth-century Poland. Their protest at that time was that there was too much rabbinic authority and tradition, and they wanted their practice to be based on direct communication with God through prayer. Storytelling is very important to the Hasidic Jews. Jerome Mintz, a Jewish scholar, wrote:

> Storytelling won an established place in the life of the earliest hasidim and it became a part of the Shabbes ritual. . . . Rebbes often wove their teachings into an extended metaphor or parable or told an illustrative tale. . . . The telling of tales can be a mystical expression on various levels. To tell tales of the tsaddikim is one means of glorifying the tsaddikim and of contacting their piety and power. . . . In this light, the hasidim believe that tales, like prayers, contain the potential to be active agents. (Mintz 1968: 4–8)

The Hasidic Jews consider storytelling to be the best way to introduce their beliefs and practices to their children.

Traditional Jews of all divisions and sects of Judaism place great importance on the cycle of life (Steinberg 1975: 132–34). Ceremonies celebrating the stages of life from birth to death are respected and practiced. Traditional stories, folktales, legends, and proverbs are commonly used for cultural transmission and the shaping of subsequent generations, and the stories often have many levels of meaning: entertainment, human interest, social examples, and moral teaching.

Jewish humor, both from within the culture and without, is a popular form of folklore. Sometimes respectful, sometimes not, it is often told in a narrative joke style, and the Jews are often demeaned by the humor. Both males and females in the Jewish tradition, generally speaking, are articulate, well-educated individuals. Jews have been misunderstood, consistently blamed for the death of the Christian divinity, Jesus Christ, and persecuted throughout much of recorded history. The heinous persecutions culminated in the Nazi Holocaust, which resulted in the tragic death of over six million Jews.

Islam

The worldwide religion of Islam was founded in Arabia in the seventh century by a prophet named Muhammad. Like the Jews, Muslims (or Moslems), the followers of Islam, believe in one God (Allah), and they believe that individuals, societies, and governments should all be obedient to the will of God. The will of God, according to the Islamic faith, is found in the Qur'an, which was revealed to Muhammad. There are over 700 million Muslims in the world, the majority of whom are Sunni. The Shiites are the largest minority group.

Because Islam spread into different parts of the world far from the founding center, folk Islam emerged among the adherents. Old and new beliefs merged, and a belief in spirits called jinn, invisible beings with supernatural power, entered the lore. The plural of the word is *jinn* or *jinna,* but "the singular is jinni, the origin of the story of the 'genie' in Aladdin's lamp" (Burke 1996: 247). Though mentioned in the Qur'an, stories of the jinn became exaggerated in folk Islam, and rituals for protection from these spirits became a part of daily life. Superstitious behaviors such as guarding against the evil eye, the use of amulets and charms, the chanting of protective sayings, and the practice of divination became common. Stories of the jinn describe them as formed of fire. They are shape-shifters and can present themselves as hideous giants. They are said to live on the mountains of Káf, which encircle the world.

The afterlife Paradise for Muslims is a place of beauty, peace, and the best of nature's bounties. To live the religion fully and earn the right to go to Paradise after mortal death, the five pillars of Islam are observed: sincere recitation of the Muslim creed of belief; formal prayer said five times a day; alms-giving; the duty to fast; and at least one pilgrimage during one's lifetime to Mecca, the center of Islamic worship. These elements, in addition to private prayer, are practiced throughout the world. The Muslims are an extremely diverse people, and their stories reflect syncretic (combined) traditions of their Muslim religious folkways and mores and those of the country or region where they live. Though formal worship services are held on Friday at noon, Muslims are expected to incorporate the practice of their faith at all times. Children, no matter where they live in the world, are taught the Arabic language and to memorize from the Qur'an from a very young age. The method of teaching is

Many stories of the *Jinn* describe them as formed of fire.

by oral recitation: children listen to simple verses and repeat them until they become familiar. In this way, both the language and the lessons of the Qur'an are integrated into their upbringing.

Christianity

Followers of the Christian belief system believe that Jesus Christ (1–33 C.E.) was the world Messiah prophesied in the Old Testament. The core of the religion is that God is the creator of all things, including humans, and that He is good. Humans, though essentially endowed with goodness, are inclined toward pride and greed. Through the guidance of the Spirit of God and the grace of Christ, believed by Christians to be the son of God, humans can be redeemed by making right choices if they focus their moral ethics and behaviors on the teachings of Christ. The death and subsequent resurrection of Christ provided an example for all humans, and through belief in that event, Christians believe that forgiveness, salvation, and eternal life are promised to them if they keep his commandments.

By the end of the first century, many of the instructions, parables, and stories of Christ were written, approved, and became accepted as the New Testament tradition in fulfillment of prophecies of the Old Testament. Through the testimonies of Jesus Christ's 12 Apostles and their followers, Christianity spread quickly through the Mediterranean world, and in 315 c.e., it was declared by the emperor Constantine to be the official religion of the Roman Empire. The teaching survived over time by the oral and written testimonies of monks. There are three major divisions of Christianity: Eastern Orthodoxy, Roman Catholic, and Protestant. Within these three traditions are countless sects and interpretations. The primary sacraments practiced by the Christian churches are baptism and communion.

The parables of Christ, traditional stories of saints, individual experience narratives, and accounts of miracles have given themes and motifs to artists throughout the centuries since Christ's life. The earliest identified examples of fables or anecdotes to which Christian morals were added are the homilies of Saint Gregory the First (around 600 c.e.). Called exempla, by the thirteenth and fourteenth centuries, Franciscan and Dominican monks had developed them into oral performances and shared them with the public in marketplaces, fairs, and other gatherings. Christianity has permeated much of the Western world's art and literature, sometime subtly and sometimes openly. Ancient Nordic stories as well as *Beowulf*, the oldest known Anglo-Saxon narrative, bear the influence of early Christian motifs.

In contemporary life, Christian storytelling takes place in both Sunday schools and parochial schools around the world. From Sunday school manuals to flannel board stories, teachers in the Christian churches continue to transmit the parables and fables found in both the Old and New Testaments of the Bible to their listeners. Protestant, Roman Catholic, and Eastern Orthodox Christians use storytelling to transmit both morality and their belief systems.

Hinduism

Hinduism is actually a Western term for a belief system that developed within the ancient historical and social system of India. Thousands of years old, it emphasizes a correct or right way of living called dharma. There is no particular founder, and there are myriad variations in gods, systems of worship, scriptures used, and festivals observed. One commonality among the many Hindu sects is the concept of transmigration or reincarnation. *Samsāra* is the term used to represent the process of birth and rebirth continuing for life after life. One's karma, or cause, determines the next life in the cycle as the next life form one finds oneself in is a consequence of one's choices in each state (Pandharipande 1996: 114).

There are rich writings related to the Hindu belief system, though none are considered as the final authority. The Vedas (1200–500 B.C.E.) are the earliest, followed by the *dharma sutra* and the *dharma shastras* (500 B.C.E.–500 C.E.), and added later were the *Ramayana* and the *Mahabharata* (which contains the *Bhagavad Gita,* one of the most influential scriptures in the Hindu belief system).

There are over 500 million Hindus, and their practices include many examples of oral, material, customary, and ritual lore. In the Hindu belief system, prose commentaries called the *Brahmanas* explain the relationship between the sacred texts (the Vedas) and the many ritual ceremonies that have been constructed to reflect the texts. Myths and stories serve to transmit the ancient messages, and throughout India, story cloths with pictures are used to tell the tales of gods, animals, warriors, various symbols, and most importantly, stories of the Mother God. The three primary Hindu gods are Shiva, Vishnu, and Brahma, and obsessive devotion among the monks and priests often results in transcendent practices of spiritual over physical needs. Festivals, based on the lunar calendar, are varied regionally, but there are general patterns of festival celebrations throughout India and also wherever there are settlements of people who follow this ancient religion.

Buddhism

The teachings of Siddhartha Gautama, in India around 2,500 years ago, resulted in the Buddhist belief system. Similar to and derived from ancient Hindu traditions, the system is summarized in four noble truths, which incorporate karma, or acts and consequences, by which good or evil deeds result in rewards or punishment in this life and in the next. The Buddhist path of enlightenment winds through morality, meditation, wisdom, and the eightfold path. As is true for Hinduism, storytelling has been an important element of this belief system, and many of the tales emphasize rebirths and former lives.

The goal is called nirvana, or an absorption of self into the infinite. The eightfold path is progressive and includes a mastery of understanding, aspiration, speech, conduct, means of livelihood, endeavor, mindfulness, and contemplation, always seeking the middle and perfectly balanced practice of these attributes. The underlying purpose of Buddhism is spiritual development and a release from human suffering.

Buddhists believe that adoption of the tenets of religion by *skillful means,* a term often used in the religion, meaning that whatever temperament or level of understanding a people might have, is acceptable. Therefore, Buddhism is a system that could be easily adapted by vastly different cultures. The popular version of Buddhism often differs greatly from the official and original teachings. Though it is impossible to give a firm number of individuals who follow Buddhism, the belief system is present and dominant in Asia, where over one billion people live.

PATHS TO UNDERSTANDING STORIES AND FOLKLORE

Over time, scholars have developed definitions and classifications to aid readers in their understanding of the vast world of expressive human culture as preserved in stories and folklore. In the next chapter, different types and uses of traditional stories and folklore will be defined. Words are used for many purposes in the human experience. They can both entertain and teach, they can uplift or curse, and they can illuminate or baffle the human mind. Understanding the many kinds of stories, their origins, and both the commonalities and differences between and among them, has been the work of many professional researchers throughout the twentieth century. The stories and lore formed of words have been made more accessible to students and their teachers by the scholars' definitions and classifications.

WORKS CITED

Agnes, Michael, ed. 2004. *Webster's New World College Dictionary.* 4th ed. Cleveland, OH: Wiley.

Auerbach, Loren. 1997. "Gods of War and Destiny." In *Sagas of the Norseman: Viking and German Myth,* 23–55. London: Duncan Baird.

Black Elk, Wallace, and William S. Lyon. 1990. *Black Elk: The Sacred Ways of a Lakota.* New York: Harper Collins.

Burke, T. Patrick. 1996. *The Major Religions: An Introduction with Texts.* Cambridge, MA: Blackwell.

Dundes, Alan. 1999. *Holy Writ as Oral Lit: The Bible as Folklore.* Oxford: Rowman and Littlefield.

Eliot, Alexander. 1990. *The Universal Myths.* New York: Truman Talley Books/ Meridian.

Goring, Rosemary, and Frank Whaling, eds. 1994. *Larousse Dictionary of Beliefs and Religions.* New York: Larousse Kingfisher Chambers.

Kassis, Hanna. 1997. "'Here I Am Lord': Preparation and Burial of the Dead." In *Life after Death in World Religions,* ed. Harold Coward, 48–65. Maryknoll, NY: Orbis Books.

Kostova, Elizabeth. 2005. *The Historian.* New York: Little, Brown.

Mintz, Jerome R. 1968. *Legends of the Hasidim: An Introduction to Hasidic Culture and Oral Tradition in the New World.* Chicago: University of Chicago Press.

Pandharipande, Rejeshwari Vijay. 1996. *The Eternal Self and the Cycle of Sams ra: Introduction to Asian Mythology and Religion.* 3d ed. Needham Heights, MA: Simon and Schuster Custom Publishing.

Roe, Betty D., Suellen Alfred, and Sandy Smith. 1998. *Teaching through Stories: Yours, Mine, and Theirs.* Norwood, MA: Christopher-Gordon.

Simpson, Jacqueline. 1997. "The Viking and Germanic World." In *Sagas of the Norsemen: Viking and German Myth,* 6–21. London: Duncan Baird.

Steinberg, Milton. 1975. *Basic Judaism.* San Diego: Harcourt Brace Jovanovich.

Sutherland, Z. 1997. *Children and Books.* 9th ed. New York: Addison-Wesley.

Taylor, Barry. "Greensleeves." Midi File 1. Available at: http://www.contemplator. com/england/grenslevs.html. Accessed 7 October 2005.

Taylor, Thomas. 1980. *The Eleusinian and Bacchic Mysteries.* San Diego, CA: Wizards Bookshelf.

Thury, Eva M., and Margaret K. Devinney. 2005. *Introduction to Mythology: Contemporary Approaches to Classical and World Myths.* New York: Oxford University Press.

Two
Definitions and Classifications

DEFINING STORY

A story is a narrative that gives an account of one or more happenings or events by arranging basic information or materials into a time sequence. It is made up of many elements including a plot, setting, theme, rising action, conflict, resolution, and usually characters or actors. A story can be true or fictitious, and it usually has a purpose of either entertaining or informing the listener or reader. A well-constructed story often makes us want to know what happens next. The plot of a story, suggested by many literary scholars to be the most important element, is what gives story a beginning, a middle, and an end. It is the sequence of events. As noted in *A Handbook to Literature,* Aristotle, in his work *Poetics,* called the plot "the arrangement of the incidents" (Harmon and Holman 1999: 393). The two primary elements of a plot are the characters and the conflict created by the author.

Many teachers of story and drama use a pyramid shape to give their students a visual image of plot and story elements. In 1863, a scholar named Gustav Freytag designed a pyramid that illustrated the structural components, or parts, of many kinds of narratives and drama. Imagine an upside-down "V." At the lower part of the left leg, Freytag suggested that a story begins with an explanation (exposition), which introduces the setting, characters, and the basic circumstances. Further up on the same side appears the concept of tension (or complication) in the story, which is created by an inciting incident of some sort. At the top of the pyramid is the climax (or high point) of the story, which occurs at the peak of interest or suspense. That is followed with a downward direction on the right leg, which is described as the turning point (a change in understanding). The turning point is followed

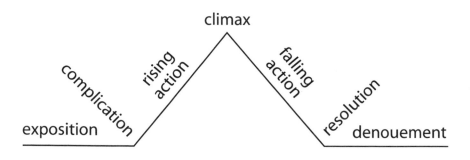

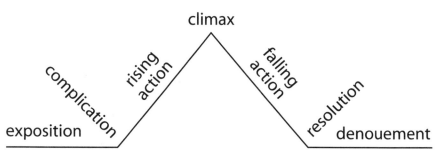

Freytag's Pyramid illustrating the structural components or parts of many kinds of narratives and drama. *Michelle Brown Design.* .

by resolution, which puts an end to the conflict. The denouement ties the story together after the conflict is resolved. The left leg of the pyramid is called "rising action" because it represents the building of the story's tension and complexity. The right leg, called "falling action," suggests that the story is coming to resolution (followed by denouement) (Freytag 1904: n.p.).

There are many kinds of stories and many uses for them. There is probably no one authority out there who can tell you exactly what a story is, or what a good story is supposed to do, but there are many voices that try to explain the purposes and complexities of story and story elements. Freytag's pyramid demonstrates how rising action, conflict, and resolution follow one another to create a narrative or drama. Characters play key roles in the development of the story, and it will be helpful to remember that in some stories, conflict is never resolved and there is no denouement or cleaning up of the loose ends. Some of the world's modern literature, short stories and novels, seem to leave the resolution of the story to the reader.

VARIOUS TYPES OF LITERATURE THAT EMPLOY STORY

Literature is the deliberate creation of an author or authors who produce imaginative prose or poetry. Because of some writers' creativity and ability to engage the readers, literature often remains in a culture for centuries. Sometimes written literature passes into the spoken lore of the people, and sometimes, the spoken or traditional lore is used to enhance or even provide the plot structure for literature. Literature can be entirely fictional or it can be interwoven with historical events and characters. Some literature has emotional effects on the readers, and the most lasting literature seems to appeal to many people on many different levels. The shared human condition causes humankind to have many experiences in common (though maybe even more differ), and to read about the experiences of others around the world, whether fictional or nonfictional, both entertains and teaches.

Literature for Entertainment

Much of our written literature, ranging from early Greco-Roman and Asian mythology and stories, to Italy's Dante (1265–1321) and Boccaccio (1313–75); England's Chaucer (1340–1400) and Shakespeare (1564–1616); and all the other great literature and drama of the world, was written primarily for entertainment. Today's condensed books and short stories in magazines, and even HBO (Home Box Office) television drama serve the same purpose. From detective novels like those featuring Sherlock Holmes to contemporary romance novels and even the Harry Potter series, literature is usually the product of an informed and fertile imagination and the business of serious publishers. Readers both need and want to be entertained with good stories, and our American bookshops are bursting with both old and new literature to meet those needs. Robert Fulford wrote: "We live under a Niagara of stories: print, television, movies, radio, and the Internet deliver to us far more stories than our ancestors could have imagined, and the number of stories available to us seems to grow larger every year" (1999: 149).

There is a distinct contrast between literature that has been created and marketed by talented writers and publishers and the literature of folktale and vernacular or oral storytelling. Literature, imagined, invented, and written by writers and journalists, is an art form recognized and appreciated by the world. Folktale and folk stories, to be authentic and legitimate, must emerge from the culture that they represent. For instance, tales of Paul Bunyan and Babe, his enormous blue ox, are entertaining stories of life in the Minnesota lumber camps, but they were created by a professional writers, which places them under the category of literature rather than folklore. Bunyan first appeared in print after being invented by a newspaperman and former logger, James McGillivray. The Bunyan figure really became well known "beginning in 1922 when another former woodsman, and advertising copywriter named W. B. Laughead, used Bunyan as the vehicle for promoting the products of the Red River Lumber Company" (Polley 1978: 356). On the other hand, stories about initiations, pranks, miracles, and other events that may emerge from the lumber camps of the West Coast, such as Oregon or Washington State, are considered authentic folklore. Both of these types of stories entertain, but one is created from imagination, and the other has emerged from lived experience.

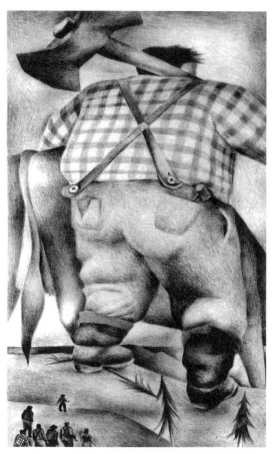

Paul Bunyan, the great logger of Minnesota.

Literature takes many forms, and it is helpful to look a little closer at how literature and folklore can work together. Young adult novels have become very popular in the United States because most of them have characters with whom their intended audience can identify. The characters are portrayed realistically enough that the readers feel and understand the presenting conflicts. Since S. E. Hinton's 1967 breakthrough novel in which the characters expressed themselves with credibility and persuasiveness using young adult slang (*The Outsiders*), themed novels with stories ranging from drug abuse, to teen pregnancy, to gang conflict have been written in the language of young people, and these stories both entertain and teach. The very slang that the teens in Hinton's books and others like them use can be categorized or classified as oral folklore. Slang, swear words, and other passing verbal fads can be considered legitimate folklore. In this we see an example of how folklore informs literature, and there will be other examples of this as we move through this text.

Literature for Didactic (Teaching) Purposes

There is a world of nonfiction literature and research, from history, anthropology, and religious studies to physics, mathematics, engineering, medicine, business, and other disciplines, which includes written and anecdotal story examples to clarify and contextualize knowledge about the topic at hand. Narratives are often used for teaching principles and points, and though many of them are passed along in a folkloric way, that is, from person to person by oral transmission, many are created and written specifically for purposes of teaching.

In religious belief systems, for instance, there are many written stories used to convey pious examples as well as simple common sense to the followers of the religion. The Roman Catholic Church, a liturgical faith (meaning that the rituals of the faith are systematic according to the calendar year), has many adherents who use a little book called *Lives of the Saints for Every Day of the Year* (Hoever 1989). Opening the book at random, the page for May 25 lists St. Mary Magdalene de Pazzi as the saint to be honored for that day. Many traditional Roman Catholics name their children according to the saint on whose birthday their child is born. St. Mary Magdalene de Pazzi was born in 1566 to a noble Florentine family and joined the Carmelite nuns when she was 17. According to the explanation, she was "endowed with the spirit of prophecy. . . . [She] found her vocation in prayer and penance for the reform of all states of life in the Church and for the conversion of all men" (210).

Included in many published collections of the *Grimms' Fairy Tales* are several stories listed under the heading of "The Children's Legends." These are a sampling of teaching stories, literary works watched over by the Roman Catholic Church for centuries to be used by way of narrative examples of faith. They were written stories to be kept intact, and they were not to be changed by oral transmission. As the late folklore scholar Max Lüthi stated: "the saint's legend is not only a story one *can* read, it is also a story one *should* read. It is believed to have the power to edify the faithful and strengthen them [the faithful reader] in their belief. It tells about the saints, from unknown local saints or their relics all the way up to Christ and Mary" (Lüthi 1976: 37). The central feature of stories collected in "The Children's Legends" is the miracle, and the stories suggest that common people, as well as those who have officially dedicated their lives to Christ and the Roman Catholic Church (priests, monks, and nuns), can have contact with God and the supernatural. One of my favorites, because it encourages acts of charity, is "God's Food," a bold and explicit story of a starving widow and her children who had appealed to her wealthy sister for sustenance and were denied because of the sister's selfishness. Just before dying with her last two living children, the widow says, "For earthly food have we no longer any desire. God has already satisfied the hunger of three of us, and he will hearken to our supplications likewise" (Stern 1972: 822).

The didactic written literature of the world, from the Hindu *Rig Veda* (ancient hymns) and Upanishads (mystical and philosophical prose works) to the Chinese *Tao Te Ching* (nuggets of philosophy for living), to the Hebrew Bible and Islamic Qur'an and many other major works, has informed human cultural behavior by teaching and shaping attitudes and social interaction. Another style of storytelling in written literature is journalistic reporting, which will be discussed in the next few paragraphs. This form of storytelling is important because it shapes human response to events of the world ranging from the local to the global.

Journalism

Terry Lee, editor of the journal *Points of Entry: Cross-Currents in Storytelling,* stated that "The leanest hard-news story stripped for speed is just as much a *narrative* as the newspaper magazine story driven by a storyline as complex in plot and characters as a family vacation in an RV. Each tells a story following time-honored narrative structures" (2003: 7). Though journalism is based on factual reporting, literary journalism "invites readers into the story to participate in the business of making meaning, and to learn something about the business of being human" (8).

Another definition for journalism, written by Betty Medsger, affirms the concept that news reporting is, essentially, storytelling: "Journalism is defined here as news and feature story gathering and storytelling in words and visual elements" (1996: 7).

In the 1990s, journalistic reporting in narrative form was labeled and identified as creative nonfiction. This is an important designation because it suggests that the writer is presenting facts but is also using artistic creativity to present the factual information. The journal *Creative Nonfiction*, published since 1993 and edited by Lee Gutkind of the University of Pittsburgh, presents articles and other texts covering diverse topics from ethnic groups to foods to astronomy. The articles and texts explain and contextualize the topics with more detail and depth including everyday experiences and interpretations in relation to the subject under discussion, but to do so, they use literary techniques used by fiction writers and poets. The perspective or point of view of the writer is reflected in the material, and there may be settings, dialogue, and specific detail. Two examples of creative nonfiction would be *Robbing the Bees: A Biography of Honey,* by Holley Bishop (2005) and *Salt: A World History,* by Mark Kurlansky (2003).

In *Robbing the Bees,* Bishop tells many stories. In one, she describes the observations of Nobel Prize–winning author Maurice Maeterlinck:

> In the beginning of the twentieth century, a Belgian dramatist named Maurice Maeterlinck studied the hive and was rewarded with poetry. He wrote *The Life of the Bee* after years of observing bees as he lived amongst them. His devotion took place in France, surrounded as he was by orchards and vineyards as he sat at a table upon which, like Aristotle, he had placed little dishes of honey to attract his muse. Using an observation hive and a pot of paint, he marked individual bees with bright dots of color and chronicled the life of the colony in lyrical, spiritual detail. Maeterlinck did not contribute scientific advances, but his little book, only 150 pages long, is a marvel of natural history writing, courtesy of the bees. (2005: 63, 64)

Thus, with careful description and specificity of detail, Bishop tells us a story about Maeterlinck's work.

In Mark Kurlansky's creative nonfiction called *Salt: A World History,* descriptions of place enhanced by sensory and pictorial detail place the reader vicariously in the presence of the rivers described:

> In the list of great rivers that played essential roles in the history of salt—the Yangtze, the Nile, the Tiber and the Po, the Elbe and the Danube, the Rhône and the Loire—a gurgling mud-bottomed waterway that flows for only seventy

miles from the English Midlands to the Irish Sea has to be included: The River Mersey. (2003: 179)

Contextualizing with descriptions like "a gurgling mud-bottomed waterway" increases both the interest and credibility of Kurlansky's creative nonfiction history of salt.

Historical Literature

Historical literature, unlike creative nonfiction, mixes facts and fiction and develops narratives by inventing characters whose stories are told within the framework of historical events. Settings can be invented also, as well as factual characters and places. These types of stories reconstruct a past age, and the formula for a historical novel is usually a plot that includes cultural conflict played out by fictional characters. Writers from the past who used this form include (among many others) James Fenimore Cooper: *The Last of the Mohicans* (1826); Lev Nikolaevich Tolstoy: *War and Peace* (1869); and Alexandre Dumas: *The Three Musketeers* (1844) and *The Count of Monte Cristo* (1844–45). Contemporary texts such as Harper Lee's *To Kill a Mockingbird* (1960) and Chris Crowe's *Mississippi Trial, 1955* (2002) treat attitudes and events from history as facts and weave them into fictional tales.

Digital Storytelling

Digital storytelling, a modern version of the ancient art of storytelling, is a technology-based method of writing. Usually two to four minutes long, it is often a first-person narrative illustrated with still photographs and featuring the voice of the person making it enhanced by music. This mode of storytelling reaches broad and diverse audiences and is being used in K–12 education, nonprofit and government agencies, and various private businesses. Digital storytelling uses the classic narrative techniques (rising action, conflict, and resolution) plus interactive digital technologies to engage its viewers. This new medium extends beyond stories and includes multiplayer games as well as wireless media and virtual reality.

Using new tools and techniques, like HTML hypertext links to the Web, animation programming, and digital moviemaking, talented writers and visual artists are using innovative, modern technology to write, tell, and illustrate their narratives. *Digital Storytelling: A Creator's Guide to Interactive Entertainment,* by Carolyn Handler Miller (2004), discusses the history and development of digital storytelling and suggests that interactive storytelling may be traced "all the way back to prehistoric religious rituals" (Miller 2004: 1).

Fan Fiction

Fan fiction (FanFic), a phenomenon of technology, is writing on the Internet that responds to and adds to published fiction. Amateur writers can create new situations or adventures for characters from movies, television shows, and popular culture. Using the Internet, e-mail lists, or newsgroups, the fans who write do not have commercial interests. These writers are often creatively enthusiastic, but their work is not always appreciated by the owners of the original works. Further information about FanFic and the answers to many questions about it can be found at the following Web site: http://chillingeffects.org/fanfic/faq.cgi.

Through the Web and Internet, for those who have become members on various sites, contact between published authors and fans is made possible, and the sites provide a place for people to access their favorite writers in order to ask questions, share stories, and find help with their own writing. Further, the fan fiction sites provide strands where in addition to creating new characters, writers may write alternative endings to published stories and in essence create their own version of the work.

Of interest to some readers might be the Harry Potter Fan Fiction Web site (http://harrypotterfanfiction.com). Representing 7,620 authors, 14,801 stories, and 60 million hits since January 2005, the site includes stories, riddles, scavenger hunts, lotteries, and even "writers' duels." With forums and links, the site is popular and fun for both interested children and adults.

The previous few pages in this chapter have described several forms of story in *written* form. The next section describes variations of oral, or vernacular, literature. Though much of oral lore and stories has been written down, its origins were in the spoken word transmitted from one person to another or from one group to another over time (diachronic study) or even occurring at different places at the same time (synchronic study). The oral folklore described here was once told by storytellers in different cultures who were called by many names: bard, troubadour, tale-bearer, teller, epic poet, singer of epic poems. Besides the official tellers, many forms of oral storytelling and folklore are passed along by people like you and me.

DEFINING ORAL FOLKLORE

Three general categories for oral, or vernacular, folklore are myth, legend, and folktale, and those categories will be described in the following pages. But before proceeding to those definitions, it is important to gain an understanding of who the "folk" we are referring to are, from a professional and academic point of view. According to the late Alan Dundes, a widely published and respected folklorist, "The term 'folk' can refer to *any group of people whatsoever* who share at least one common factor" (Dundes 1989: 11). The "common factor" might be nationality, religion, occupation, or language. As professional folklorists describe "folk," neither economic status, urban or rural heritage, nor political or cultural persuasion excludes anyone from being a part of the folk. Whether a highly educated nuclear physicist, an under-educated food vendor at the beach or ball park, or a person challenged with intellectual disabilities, we are all "folk."

Several decades ago, folklorist William Bascom defined the forms of oral folklore in an important and still quoted essay called "The Forms of Folklore: Prose Narratives" (1965). He does not claim originality in the essay, but he suggests that the definitions he presents "conform to what students of the folklore of both nonliterate and European societies have found" (3). He wrote: "*Prose Narrative,* I propose, is an appropriate term for the widespread and important category of verbal art which includes myths, legends, and folktales. These three forms are related to each other in that they are narratives in prose, and this fact distinguishes them from proverbs, riddles, ballads, poems, tongue twisters, and other forms of verbal art" (3). Bascom suggests that myth, legend, and folktale are not the only categories of prose narrative. Reminiscences or anecdotes and jokes may be fourth and fifth categories, but at the time Bascom wrote the article, he suggested that even these could be listed as "sub-types of the folktale and the legend" (5).

Myth

"*Myths are prose narratives which, in the society in which they are told, are considered to be truthful accounts of what happened in the remote past*" (Bascom 1965: 4; emphasis in original). Most folklorists consider myth as a sacred narrative or story set long ago in the prehistoric or timeless, ancient "long ago." Sometimes people use the word *myth* to describe something that is untrue, but most contemporary folklorists suggest that myths are the tales people tell about the origin or beginning of things. Carl Lindahl proposes that "Perhaps the most common understanding attached to the word *myth* is 'the other group's narrative religion'" (Lindahl, McNamara, and Lindow 2002: 283). Religious groups usually regard their foundation or beginning stories as truth, but outsiders often define the stories as mythic traditions, which implies that they are believed but are possibly not literally true. Myths, as defined by folklorists, are often accompanied by ritual and usually have supernatural elements. They are explanatory and can describe the creation of the world, animal characteristics, how gods and humans came to be, and early customs, rituals, and regulatory boundaries of a society. Most cultures around the world have traditional mythic stories and traditions.

One of the best-known collections of myths in studies of the Western world comes from the ancient Greek and Roman traditions. It is interesting to note that the ancient Greeks did not have a word for myth. Their stories about gods and heroes came to be called "myths" by others studying their corpus (body) of work when looking back over time, even across centuries, that had already passed. The Greek word *mythos* originally meant a word, story, or speech. In ancient Greece, approximately 500 B.C.E., scholars made a distinction between the terms *logos* (rational, knowledgeable speech) and *mythos* (make-believe or fiction). Over time, the mythos or *mythoi* came to define fantastic or fictional stories rather than orally transmitted origin stories. Myths have served to determine social behavior in groups by creating boundaries and structures through the use of the prose narratives; that is, the ordinary form of written or spoken language rather than poetry.

The structure and function of myth, as explained by mythologist Mircea Eliade, has five characteristic qualities. First, myth tells the history of action taken by supernatural powers. Second, the history represented by the myth is considered to be absolutely true and sacred by the group whose origins it explains. Third, it is always related to creation because it tells how something came into existence or how patterns of behaviors (or the functioning of societies) came into being. Fourth, by knowing the myths, ritual ceremonies and practices in harmony with the myths can be recounted or performed. Fifth, members of a society live the myths by becoming influenced by the power of the events recollected or reenacted (1975: 18, 19).

Legend

"Legends are prose narratives which, like myths, are regarded as true by the narrator and his audience, but they are set in a period considered less remote, when the world was much as it is today" (Bascom 1965: 4; emphasis in original). A legend is defined as a story that may have a trace of history within it. Legends often carry traditional concepts and are not set in the remote past like myths. They are usually not based on religion or sacred themes; however, as mentioned above, there are children's legends that are related to religious miracles and traditions, and some legends have supernatural elements within them. Legends are often localized, that is presented as a true account emergent from a specific region. Because of this, some legends express the national spirit of some countries. Characters in legends are usually human, and the legends often express the values held by the

group from which the legend emerged. Legends, which are historical and traditional oral prose narratives, describe past heroes, wars, migrations, victories and even defeats. Sometimes involving the unseen, legends, as Bascom stated, may also include "local tales of buried treasure, ghosts, fairies and saints" (5).

Medieval legends often contain multiple episodes about a single figure or event. These groups of legends are sometimes referred to as "legend cycles." The Celtic or even Continental legends of King Arthur and the knights of the round table are often labeled the "Arthurian Cycle," while certain stories from the region of Ulster in Northern Ireland are often referred to as the "Ulster Cycle." These groups of legends are sometimes referred to as singular, for example, as the legend of Arthur, but the reality is that they are made up

King Arthur and his Knights of the Round Table.

of many legends, each relating to a central figure or to an event related to the central figure or location (Tangherlini 2002: 241).

Another type of legend, very popular in contemporary society worldwide, is called the urban legend. These are also referred to as contemporary or modern legends or even urban myths. These legends are prose narratives usually reported as true experiences of individuals, but as they are passed from person to person, by word-of-mouth, the Internet, newspapers or other printed materials, radio, and/or television, they establish *variants* (varied versions with the same core) and often creatively increase in complexity and interest. Their origins are generally impossible to trace, and because of that they have been nicknamed "friend-of-a-friend" or FOAF lore. In some ways, urban legends change a little like the sentence or phrase changes in the "telephone game," in which a sentence is whispered to someone in the front of the first row of a classroom (or whatever setting) and then whispered from person to person up and down the rows until it at last reaches the person sitting in the last seat of the last row, who speaks it aloud. In its final form, the sentence is almost always something very different than the original. Even so, it usually contains some traces of the original.

Urban lore is much like that. It changes with the telling, and many of the examples are so credible that it is easy to be deceived by them. On the other hand, there are usually fallacies that reveal clues to the lore's fictitious intent. Stories like finding a breaded and deep-fried mouse or rat in a bucket of Kentucky Fried Chicken or of thieves stealing human kidneys to sell on the black market as organ replacements have become widely circulated examples of this legend genre. Jan Brunvand, a folklorist who has gathered and published many examples of urban lore sent to him from all over the world, suggests that "Basic modern anxieties often lie behind popular urban legends. An instance of this is fear of contamination from manufactured goods" (1998: 209). In a highly industrialized and often impersonal world, stories like these circulate as entertainment, cautionary or warning tales, and as simple anecdotes about others' experiences. When you hear a very unusual story or legend of this sort, reflect and rehearse the different elements of the tale in your mind before accepting it as literal truth. The teller may have conveyed it to you in all sincerity, but *you* may be able to find the fallacies.

Folktale

"Folktales are prose narratives which are regarded as fiction" (Bascom 1965: 4; emphasis in original). Folktales are structured stories, usually called *Märchen* by scholars, that have either human or animal characters. Brunvand wrote that their "characteristic features . . . are formularized language and structure,

supernatural motifs, and sympathy for the underdog or commoner" (1998: 235). These are often, but not always, the "Once upon a time" and "Happily ever after" stories common in the Western world, but they are also present in all cultures and are used for many purposes. They are passed from generation to generation from place to place, and their settings can be in any region or country at any time. They are secular, or nonreligious, but they serve various purposes in maintaining traditions through the expressive culture of many communities worldwide.

Folktale can carry multiple threads of meaning, and it is often part of every-day conversation as well as being reserved for particular use in teaching traditions and boundaries, cultural legacies, and amusement. In many cultures, folktale serves all of these purposes and even more. The tales not only teach about cultural mores and basic beliefs, but they also validate ways of life and even serve as an "escape mechanism" in times of stress (Bascom 1954: 344).

From bedtime tales for children to campfire ghost stories for teens, to complex jokes, to story anecdotes (and even gossip) shared by adults, folktale is structured in traditional narrative style and has a beginning, a middle, and an end. From the complex and humorous tales of Coyote told by the Navajo and Pueblo tellers, to the sage, didactic use of folktale by the Hasidic Jews, to the entertaining and engaging folktale traditions of Oceania, Asia, Europe, and Scandinavia, these tales traverse the world. Because thousands of folktale variants exist, and because of similar motifs, structures, and strands within them, scholars have worked for decades to gather, classify, and discuss the ways in which many of the tales are both similar and dissimilar and to discover the possible historical connections and links between them. Tale-types and motifs have been categorized and made accessible to interested investigators, and later in this chapter some of the complicated but scholarly work of typing and categorizing will be presented and explained. These indices may become useful tools for your study of the ubiquitous folktale.

VARIATIONS OF PROSE NARRATIVES

Folklorists, mythologists, and storytellers have classified many kinds of oral lore. Names for the various classifications vary among professional schol-ars, but the following list describes many well-known forms and categories of oral folklore. Many collections have been made over time, and examples of these and other forms of oral folklore can easily be found in various texts and even folklore archives where university student collections are often kept permanently for reference and research. Storytellers (often called "tellers" in modern culture) search many avenues for materials to share with their varied audiences. Knowing the following classifications and designations helps to determine the appropriate use of stories when choosing and preparing them for performance and presentation.

Complex Tales

You probably have some recollection of the time when you progressed in reading from storybooks to chapter books. For most young readers, this takes place around third or fourth grade. Complex tales are more likely to be found in chapter books because they are designed to be more challenging to follow, and they use different elements of the story in different ways. The reader or listener must be focused and engaged with the text or performance in order to remember the parts. In complex tales, a skilled storyteller may move backward and forward in time and space and will weave several events and episodes together. The story might have the same characters in different settings, or possibly the same setting with different characters and varied situations. Fairy tales or Märchen (further explained below), religious tales (faith-promoting episodic tales or legends), and novellas (stories about events and complicated human relationships and situations in the real world) are complex tales. A story like that of Robin Hood, the bandit who stole from the rich and gave to the poor in England's medieval Sherwood Forest, is a complex tale. The story progresses, and the reader accumulates information as the story unfolds. It is a complex process, and the complexity itself is one of many elements that storytellers use to engage the audience.

In the ancient world, storytellers or bards who often traveled from court to court, or village to village, told complex book-length stories that were later written in both poetic and prose forms. These were complex tales, multilayered with characters, settings, and events. The bards memorized these ancient, now well-known epics like the Sumerian *Gilgamesh,* Homer's *Iliad* and *Odyssey,* the Old English *Beowulf,* the East Indian *Ramayana,* and many others. In the ancient times, a bard or poet could not use a tape recorder to help listen to the tale over and over again in order to know and understand it well and memorize it, so formulaic devises were created. These relaters of stories found patterns for the telling to help them remember and tell their tales in ways that would illuminate the story, make it credible and convincing, create visual imagery and almost tactile experiences among the listeners, and importantly, help them remember all of it. Many tellers today choose complex tales to share, and they prepare carefully, rehearsing before each telling, so that the multiple episodes and layers of the stories could be linked together for the listener's understanding and edification.

In John Maier's discussion of Gilgamesh of Urak, he suggests that the episodes of this ancient complex tale recorded in poetic form varied from translation to translation. He stated,

> I have argued that a reading [or telling] of the poem that connects episodes that were either very different or completely absent from earlier versions of Gilgamesh stories enables us to add Disuri, Utnapishtims' wife, and the prostitute Shamhatu to the list. The goddesses and humans who assist Enkidu and Gilgamesh along the way do, largely, disappear from view once their role is fulfilled (2002: 33).

We learn from Maier's discussion that this epic story, a long and complex tale like many others, is likely to have been read and told in many ways over time, and the teller could vary it according to his or her reading and interpretation. The consequence of these variations are variants of the tale, and storytellers today often create their own versions of the complex tales they tell.

Märchen and Conte Fabulaire

Both these terms, the first German and the second French, refer to short tales. There are many similar terms that seem to have approximately the same meaning: for instance, magic tale, wonder tale, hero tale, and ordinary tale. Märchen literally means "little short story" in German, and *conte fabulaire* means "fabulous tale" in French. Both designations refer to complex stories set in a world of make-believe or fantasy, and these stories appear in children's books throughout the world. They have been used as the basic story of animated films and are often used by both professional and nonprofessional storytellers.

The stories have multiple episodes, high adventure, and often include magic. A typical Märchen or *conte fabulaire* begins with "Once upon a time" and ends with the familiar "And they all lived happily ever after." Tales such as "Snow White" or "Cinderella" have many variants in different countries and cultures, but they fit this category because of their short length, multiple episodes, adventurous style, and the use of magic. The story line is often adapted to regional settings, characters, names, and dialects, and the tales are used mostly for entertainment rather than for education. Many of the little stories, however, have been carefully examined and subjected to careful analysis to discern psychological, cultural, or symbolic meanings in the texts.

The term *Märchen* is used because the first important published collection of stories of this type was made by the brothers Grimm: Wilhelm (1785–1863) and Jacob (1786–1859) in Germany. The brothers published *Kinder- und*

Cinderella and the birds that helped with her tasks.
New York Public Library, Astor, Lenox, and Tilden Foundations.

Hausmärchen (Children's and Household Tales) in 1812, and that initial publication was followed by several more in different countries and languages. An American folklorist, Simon Bronner, reminds us that:

> Before the Grimms published their annotated collection, European folktales had received literary notice most notably from the work of Charles Perrault in France (1697) and Giambattista Basile (1637) in Italy. Among the tales given in both were Cinderella, Sleeping Beauty, and Puss in Boots. The French volume drew attention to Little Red Riding Hood, Bluebeard, and Hop o' My Thumb, while the Italian included Snow White and Beauty and the Beast. (Bronner 1998: 192)

Another use for the term *Märchen* is that of a short allegory (a narrative with meaning beyond the literal story). Writers in the 1800s, such as Johann Wolfgang von Goethe (1749–1842), Novalis (pen name of Friedrich Leopold von Hardenberg (1772–1801), Johann Ludwig Tieck (1773–1853), and Ernst Theodor Amadeus Hoffman (1776–1822) wrote *Kunstmärchen* (art tales) that were mini-fantasies with multiple meanings.

Fables

A fable is a very short story that has a moral message told in disguise. Carl Lindahl wrote that, "Generally speaking, the fable, of learned origin and cultivated by clerics, is written to cultivate a moral message" (Simonsen 2002: 13). The fable characters are often animals, but sometime inanimate objects and humans can also be central to the story. When the characters are all animals, a fable is sometimes called a beast fable or beast tale. These little narratives are often satires that point out the frequent foolishness of human choice. Joseph Jacobs wrote that "In Greece, during the epoch of the Tyrants, when free speech was dangerous, the Fable was largely used for political purposes" (Jacobs 1966: xv).

Some of the most well known fables in the Western world are those of Aesop, a Greek slave who lived in Samos about 600 B.C.E. The origin of his fables was possibly India, but he may have used them both to teach and to entertain. Very little is known about Aesop except for a few lines written by Herodotus, an ancient historian. Supposedly Aesop "flourished around 550 B.C.; was killed in accordance with a Delphian oracle; and that *wergild* [a price paid to the family of a person who has been killed by the person responsible for the death in order to atone for the killing and avoid retribution] was claimed for him by the grandson of his master, Iadmon" (Jacobs 1996: xvi). A fictional biography of Aesop called "The Life and Fables of Aesop" (second/third century C.E.) is said to have contained a collection of fables in alphabetical order. That early text was lost, but

> . . . the fables survive in a form known as the *Collectio Augustana,* named after the manuscript through which scholars first became acquainted with the book. . . . The oldest manuscripts indicate that it originally contained 231 fables (plus a further 13, which are, however, only found in the *recensio la* [revisions] of the collection), but some of these could quite conceivably have been added later. (Holzberg 2002: 4)

Aesop's fables have been preserved and used for centuries for their literary value, language study, continued pursuit of their origin, and as source

Aesop, a Greek slave, sharing his fables with children.

material and inspiration for other works. Following is an example of one of Aesop's fables.

The Mountain in Labour

A mountain was once greatly agitated. Loud groans and noises were heard; and crowds of people came from all parts to see what was the matter. While they were assembled in anxious expectation of some terrible calamity, out came a mouse.

Moral: Don't make much ado about nothing. (Aseop 1998: 14)

Another popular fable writer was La Fontaine (1621–95), a seventeenth-century Frenchman. His fables were funny, delicate, and witty, and they were said to send different messages to differently aged listeners. The fox who managed to win a piece of cheese from another animal is one of his famous stories, and it was patterned after one of the older Aesop tales. The moral of that one: "Every flatterer lives at the expense of his listeners" (Hornstein, Edel, and Frenz 1973: 291).

The Uncle Remus stories, gathered and published by American journalist and writer Joel Chandler Harris (1848–1908), may also be classified as beast fables. Though the stories often represent a weaker but usually triumphant brother rabbit as the protagonist and may be classified by some scholars strictly as animal tales, messages embedded in the fables convey the sly wisdom of slaves in the Deep South from whom Harris, as a young boy, first heard the tales. Harris eventually wrote a column in the Atlanta, Georgia, *Constitution,* and though "Harris presented Remus as content with slavery, the tales he tells themselves belie this" (Polley 1978: 260).

Uncle Remus was a plantation storyteller who shared the entertaining animal tales of Brer Rabbit and other characters.

Animal Tales

Animal tales are often told for comic and entertainment purposes, but like the Uncle Remus stories, they have also been used for teaching cultural principles and mores to children. From the medieval tales of the trickster Reynard the Fox, to the humorous contemporary cartoons of animated animals such as Bugs Bunny, the Road Runner, and even Snoopy, these tales continue to entertain us and reflect the foibles of human nature.

According to Michéle Simonsen, "Preachers [in the Middle Ages] often employed animal tales in their sermons, first exploiting the entertaining features of the folktale to gain attention of the audience and then shaping the tale to underscore moral points" (Simonsen 2002: 14). Animal tales used this way were called exempla, and they were particularly popular in France and Spain.

The Reynard the Fox stories (originally *Roman de Renart*) have provided many root plots and motifs for animal tales that followed. The stories, written in what were called "branches" rather than segments or chapters, included both animals and human characters. Stories developed out of other stories and ranged from races, to trickery about food, to freezing a wolf's tail, which causes him to lose it.

Animal tales often involve clever twists in which the underdog ends up as the winner. Folk and fairy tales such as "Beauty and the Beast" (Madame Le Prince de Beaumont), "The Frog King" and "Iron Heinrich" (both collected by Jacob and Wilhelm Grimm), and "East of the Sun and West of the Moon" (Asbjørnsen and Moe) mix animals and humans in complex tales in which communication and even commitment occur between a beast and a redemptive female (Hallett and Karasek 1996: 123).

In the Americas among the Southwestern American Indian tribes, animal stories are numerous. Told for entertainment, teaching, and cultural shaping and maintenance, there are stories about Coyote, Spider, Skunk, Ant, and many other animals. There are cultural taboos associated with some of these animal stories, particularly in the Navajo and Pueblo traditions. Both Coyote and Spider stories are only to be told in the cold months of the year (December through March) or the harmony of nature could possibly be disturbed.

Trickster Tales

Tales with trickster figures develop ambiguous characters who pull pranks in a spirit of mischief and consistently have an inconsistent mixture of innocence and malicious intent.

Often the trickster tales expose human foibles and serve as revealing cultural tales of tension and opposition. B. A. Botkin wrote that the trickster figure "has also inspired countless pranks and tricks that are part of the folkways and folk humor of everyday life from the wild-goose chases and ridiculous deceptions of April Fool's Day to what Governor Bob Taylor calls the 'eternal war between the barefooted boy and the whole civilized world'" (Botkin 1989: 358–59).

There are scholars who have built their professional careers studying the role of the trickster in society over eons of time. Paul Radin (1883–1959) was one of these, and in 1955 he wrote a text in which he discussed the trickster figure in American Indian mythology. His description of the trickster still stands among those most noted:

> Trickster is at one and the same time creator and destroyer, giver and negator, he who dupes others and who is always duped himself. He wills nothing consciously. At all times he is constrained to behave as he does from impulses over which he has no control. He knows neither good nor evil yet he is responsible for both. He possesses no values, moral or social, is at the mercy of his passions and appetites, yet through his actions all values come into being. But not only he, so our myth tells us, possesses these traits. So, likewise, do the other figures of the plot connected with him: the animals, the various supernatural beings and monsters, and man. (1972: 195–211)

French author Charles Perrault wrote a story called "Puss in Boots." It is one in which the trickster cat figure manages to gain a fortune for his young master through trickery and is an example of a classic trickster tale. Another is a Navajo trickster story told by Barre Toelken which has a "plot . . . that with the aid of Skunk, Coyote plays dead so that he can kill and eat some prairie dogs" (Georges and Jones 1995: 294). Other examples of trickster tales are continuing films like *The Matrix* (1999), *The Matrix Reloaded* (2003), and *The Matrix Revolution* (2003). Many of the complex, ambiguous characters in these stories fit Radin's description of the trickster.

Scholars of the trickster, William Hynes and William Doty, build on Radin's scholarship in a collection of essays in which the trickster emerges as a comic figure who challenges serious cultural values. Distortions play an important part in messages carried by the trickster tales, and T. O. Beidelman, one of the scholars included in the Hynes and Doty collection, states: "tact is distorted into guile, the quest for security and esteem is distorted into greed and envy, and single-minded dedication is distorted into ruthlessness" (1993: 183).

The trickster figure is difficult to define because its behavior is so various. Roger Abrahams wrote:

Trickster is . . . the most paradoxical of all characters in Western narrative—at least as far as the Western mind is concerned—for he combines the attributes of many other types that we tend to distinguish clearly. At various times he is clown, fool, jokester, initiate, culture hero, even ogre. . . . He is the central character for which we usually consider many different types of folk narratives (1968: 170–71).

Folk Narrative

When an orally transmitted prose story has been repeated at least twice with some minor or major variation, it is called a folk narrative. The discussion previous to this one explained the function of the trickster figure. In an oral performance of a trickster tale, if the main character is a coyote in Arizona, and possibly the story is violent and being told to adults, the same story would be adjusted when sharing it with young children. The core story, in a sense, belongs to the teller, and it may be changed according to the audience, setting, or time.

Folklorist Linda Kinsey Adams explained:

. . . a storyteller must always take into account the context in which she or he is performing a narrative. Storytellers may shorten or fill out their narratives to fit the needs and expectations of their audience. For example, a man who delights in recounting a particular hunting adventure to his circle of friends may produce a much more elaborated version of the same story to a group of interested outsiders. This new audience cannot be counted on to understand the allusions to local terrain, personalities, and hunting practices that would be common knowledge among the teller's friends. These new listeners must be "filled in" about important background if the story is to be effective. (Adams 1990: 23)

Folk narratives, like other stories, have a beginning, middle, and end, and the topics may range from simple gossip and tale bearing about people to stories about events to fully developed, complex tales. Oral folk narratives can be performed or presented in many ways. They can be performed through speaking, singing, acting and dancing, and many have been written. Most of the items in the definitions list you are reading now can be categorized as long or short folk narratives.

Personal Narrative

Told in first person, the personal narrative conveys a story from the personal experience of the teller. The account is shaped by combining elements that were a part of the storyteller's original experience. Often additions or enhancements are included that the individual may consider improve the narrative, and it is seldom told twice in exactly the same way. Both by the elements of the experiences selected to tell, and by the way the story is told, the personal narrative reveals much concerning the ethics and values of the teller. Layered meanings of the personal narrative can be found through careful analysis of the elements presented.

Sandra Dolby-Stahl defined this genre in a few words: "The personal narrative is a prose narrative relating a personal experience; it is usually told in first person and its content is nontraditional" (Dolby 1977: 20; 1989: 12). In a chapter called "Manipulation of Personal Experience," scholar Linda Dégh stated:

> The telling of a personal narrative is a social act, as is any other narration. It has its rules and strategies. Tellers reach their appropriate audience using communal (traditional) means to succeed in their goal: personal gratification, identity presentation, status elevation, or other, while the listeners expectation is met. This means that the manner of telling, is the choice of words, phraseology, stylistic turns, emphases, must follow the local etiquette, fitting the referential framework shaped by tradition. (Dégh 1995: 75)

The teller shapes the personal narrative to the audience, the time, and the place. Selecting, adding, deleting, and presenting the personal story consistently results in the tale being told in exactly the same way twice. The telling of the narrative creates a certain intimacy between the teller and the listener, and Dégh reminds us that "People tell personal narratives to be listened to" (39).

Novella

The novella is a short folktale that has its setting in the real world rather than in a fantasy world. Unlike the whimsical creations and recreations of the Märchen, the novella represents human beings in various settings and situations. Early Italian and French writers used this form, and many of those plots and story lines were borrowed by English writers. Shakespeare, for instance, used the novella style to incorporate short stories within the larger frameworks of some of his plays.

Frame Tale

A frame tale is a story within a story. For instance, Shakespeare's *Midsummer Night's Dream* has within it Ovid's story of "Pyramus and Thisbe" performed by the laborers. Another example is the series of tales told night after night in the ancient Arabian story tale of the *Thousand and One Nights*. In that story an easily bored king kills each of his brides after one night together. Princess Scheherazade successfully outwits him by telling a new tale with an unfinished ending each night. The king would keep her alive until the next day so she could tell him the remainder of the tale. In the end, he decides she is so clever that he does not kill her and keeps her as his wife for the rest of their lives.

The frame tale was very commonly used by writers in the late nineteenth century and early twentieth century. Frame tales written in that period include Rudyard Kipling's "The Man Who Would Be King" and Mark Twain's "Jim Baker's Blue Jay Yarn." Joel Chandler Harris used the style in the Uncle Remus stories. The overall story is considered the frame, and telling the smaller stories within the frame makes the narrative a frame tale.

Formula Tale

The formula tale depends on a set structure of plot, character, setting, and language that repeats a pattern as the narrative is presented. Used largely by storytellers for entertainment, the unfolding of the tale is repetitive, predictable, and sometimes very long. A song familiar in North America that uses the formulaic style is "Old McDonald Had a Farm," in which the verse is repeated again and again adding a new animal with each repetition. A familiar formula tale, similar to the song, is "The House That Jack Built." Repeating the verses, consistently adding an element each time the main stanza is completed, may continue until the listeners demand for it to stop.

Ballad

The ballad is a form of poetry or verse generally sung but sometimes recited. It presents a simple, sometimes dramatic, narrative, and its existence is very old. "The tradition of composing story-songs about current events and personages has been common for a long time. Hardly an event of national interest escapes being made the subject of a so-called *ballad*" (Harmon and Holman 1999: 50).

Folklorist Barre Toelken sometimes referred to the ballad as "folksong poetry," and he stated that "[it] thrives on familiarity, on repetition, and on the everyday conventions and usages of people who share close familial, social, and cultural ties" (1995: 1). The ballad uses the same melody for each stanza and tells its story in short stanzas and simple worlds. Most simply put, ballads are songs that tell stories. Georges and Jones suggest that two different criteria are important to the presentation of a ballad, "*what a ballad singer's objective is* (to tell a story) and *how she or he accomplishes that objective* (by singing)" (1995: 104; emphasis in original).

Proverb

A proverb is a short, traditional saying that expresses a perception of truth about human behavior. Often used to teach common sense life principles, these little sayings emerge in all human culture. The proverb is so various that it is almost impossible to define. Archer Taylor, an expert scholar of proverbs, stated: "Let us be content with recognizing that a proverb is a saying current among the folk" (1985: 3).

Some proverbs have been repeated so many times in different settings and cultures that the sayings simply exist in the common culture. Proverbs like: *Live and learn; Mistakes will happen; Them as has gets; Enough is enough; Haste makes waste;* and *What's done's done* occur in every age, and, as Taylor wrote: "The simple truths of life have been noted in every age, and it must not surprise us that one such truth has a long recorded history while another has none"(5).

Proverbs pass from language to language and are preserved by oral tradition. Jan Brunvand stated that "A proverb is a popular *saying* in a relatively *fixed form* [little change] that is, or has been in oral circulation" (1998: 92).

Memorate

A memorate is a folk narrative that gives a firsthand account of an experience with the supernatural. Carl W. von Syndow created the term *memorate,* which, for the most part, describes otherworldly encounters with ghosts or spirits. Sometimes an unusual encounter with a nonsupernatural creature, perhaps a perceived monster of some sort, might be called a secular memorate. Though the encounter might be repeated by others, it is usually remembered and told most often by the individual who experienced it.

Sometimes the story is so remarkable and repeated so many times that it becomes a legend of sorts. Human beings are often inclined to be gullible; that is, they believe things without completely sorting out the related facts. Writers and tellers have intentionally blurred the boundaries between the natural and supernatural, or the seen and unseen, as a narrative technique since before written records. To convincingly describe a personal experience with someone or something from the mysterious other side draws many interested readers and listeners. Sometimes the encounters are said to be with relatives or friends (revenants), or the story may be built around traditional supernatural characters (angels, devils, or other disembodied spirits). Often those who believe they have had these experiences are convinced of the literal truthfulness of their tale. That confidence in the teller impresses belief of the tale upon others.

Humorous Anecdote

When Mason L. Weems created the fictional short story about George Washington and the purported chopping down of his father's cherry tree in Washington's biography, he (Weems) had created what is called by folklorists a humorous anecdote (Weems 1976: 12, 13).

The humorous anecdote is usually short and presents an incident, or so-called incident, in the life of a historical character. American presidents, politicians, and even criminals (outlaws in the Old West and Depression Era gangsters) are often the subjects of these anecdotes. This is because they have become public figures through media presentation, and the general population (or mass public) enjoys laughing at the foibles of the famous and powerful.

Tall Tale

Jan Brunvand suggests that the success of a tall tale depends on a "willingness to lie and be lied to while keeping a straight face" (1986: 202). A tall tale creates or perpetuates a hoax by coloring a realistic story with outrageous exaggeration. Mark Twain was an American master of the tall tale, and writing from an easterner's perspective, he described episodes in the American West that still amuse readers. "The Notorious Jumping Frog of Calaveras County" is one of his most famous stories. It describes a frog jumping contest using common language and a common Western motif, buckshot, to create a funny but tense, competitive event.

The humorous tall tale was common on the American frontier with stories circulating freely about Davy Crockett, Mike Fink, and the invented literary stories of Paul Bunyan. Tall tales are not new, neither are they limited to American use. In the sixteenth-century, Frenchman Philippe d'Alcripe wrote the comedic *La Nouvelle fabrique des excellents traits de vérité* (The New Factory of Excellent Drafts of Truth), which contained many exaggerated tales. R. E. Raspe, in the eighteenth century, rewrote the German *Adventures of*

Baron Münchausen (Hieronymous Karl Friedrich, Freiherr von Münchausen of Bodenwerder, Brunswick, Germany 1720–97), also named *Baron Münchausen's Narratives of His Marvelous Travels and Campaigns in Russia*, in high literary style. Gerald Thomas wrote that "Raspe's literary redactions [revisions] became so popular that the Baron's name became a byword for tall-tale heros" (1996: 701).

Tall tales may be about heroes past or present, unusual items encountered in travel (fruits or vegetables, unusual animals, peculiar earth formations, human disfigurements), hunting and/or fishing expeditions, or just about anything else. The tall tale as a folk narrative is sometimes known as a windy, a whopper, or simply a lie. Thomas stated:

> The tall tale is generally transmitted in oral tradition in two ways: second hand, as when a person attributes an exploit or an experience to another party who originally told the tale as a personal experience—this is how most tall tales have been recorded by collectors—and first hand, as when the collector is fortunate enough to participate in a natural tale-telling session. (700)

The tall tale, as an entertaining folk narrative, is a common part of oral folklore in many informal and formal settings. From campfire circles to occupational surroundings, and from front porch lie swapping to storytelling festivals, the humorous tall tale and yarn-swapping practice continues because of the fertile imaginations of the tellers. Typical of the oral tradition, the tales change with the telling, and in a way the tales grow taller and more fun as time goes by.

Joke

A joke is a short folk narrative with an unexpected climatic punch line. Knock-knock jokes, parodies of common nursery rhymes, songs, and ballads (such as "Mary Had a Little Lamb" or "Happy Birthday"), computer circulated jokes, facetious (or scurrilous) questions relating to politics or public figures, age-related jokes, regional and traveler's jokes, as well as ethnic and nationalistic jokes abound in oral and written culture. A joke cycle commonly occurs when a popular joke format is adapted and people invent new versions. For instance, variations on jokes about blonds or about how to change a light bulb are common, and these kinds of jokes provide a means for light, conversational interaction. A fixed-form joke may be told in the same way but in different settings; that is, a joke about the size of feet told in Arkansas may be told exactly the same way in Georgia with only the location changed.

Jokes can also serve as a safety valve for society. After or even during calamities and disasters such as the terrorist attacks of September 11, 2001, the AIDs epidemic, the tsunami tragedy of December 26, 2004, wars and rumors of war, and other uncontrollable events, people use jokes in an anxiety relief function. Many of these kinds of jokes are offensive to people because they can be told at the expense of others. Even so, they continue as a release for tension. Further, some jokes also serve as release valves for hostility and aggression. A good joke, well chosen and well told, can also diffuse hostility and conflict. It is important in this case, as always, to get the punch line exactly correct!

Catch Joke

Sometimes called catch riddles, catch tales, or catch questions, the "catch" genre plays a trick on the listeners. The joke triggers a question from the listener to which the teller gives an answer that leaves the listener feeling foolish, embarrassed, or hoaxed. A wordless joke that works this way is when someone standing behind another taps the person's shoulder on the right side and then moves to the left as the receiver of the tap shifts his or her head in the direction of the tap. The tapper has moved to the other side of the receiver, and the receiver is fooled.

A storyteller might used catch riddles and jokes to initially capture the attention of an audience; however, if the joke is too harsh, it may create an uninterested group rather than an engaged one.

Riddle

A riddle is an exchange of question and answer not for the purpose of gaining information but rather to play. The questioner knows the answer but challenges the riddle slover who must create an answer. Riddles have served many purposes over time, and they have been used in literature all over the world. A riddle can range from a child's simple conundrum, that is, a riddle that contains a pun (What's black and white and red all over?—answer: a newspaper), to complex riddles posed to prospective bridegrooms to prove their intelligence, an occasional Middle Eastern practice that has been picked up and used in both the literature and drama of the world.

One type of riddle well known to folklorists is the neck-riddle, so called because a person's life (or neck) may depend on it. For instance, one neck-riddle might be about a condemned prisoner who wins his or her freedom by posing a riddle to the judge who cannot answer it because the answer is embedded in the prisoner's knowledge and experience. A fairy tale example of this is the story of Rumpelstiltskin's "What is my name?"

Jan Brunvand explained the operation of a riddle by stating:

> . . . two basic parts of a true riddle were called by [Archer] Taylor the *description* and the *block,* and they may be observed in a great variety of texts. Many riddles have only these two parts plus an answer, as in the following:
>
> > Robbers came to our house and we were all in; [description]
> >
> > the house leapt out the windows and we were all taken. [block]
>
> Answer: Fish in a net (The "house" is the water; "windows" are holes in the net). (Brunvand 1986: 91)

Rhymes

When the end or terminal sounds of lines are in exact repetition, for instance, fox and box, then the language used is said to rhyme. The repetition of like sounds at regular intervals creates the form of a stanza.

A complex topic, various familiar rhymes have been used in literature, drama, and storytelling performances over time throughout the world. Children's rhymes, or nursery rhymes, are "brief verses often anonymous and traditional, with percussive rhythm and frequent heavy rhyme" (Harmon and Holman 1999: 355). The first printed collection of children's rhymes, *Mother Goose's Melody,* appeared in England between 1781 and 1791, and "its compiler was either John Newbery, his stepson, or grandson" (Tucker 1998: 459). The first American *Mother Goose* was published in Worcester, Massachusetts, in 1785 by Isaiah Thomas. Mother Goose collections have been steadily produced both in England and the United States since the early 1800s.

Limericks

The limerick is orally circulated folk poetry, often, but certainly not always, off color. It has a definite pattern with five lines in which the first, second, and fifth rhyme; the third and fourth lines also rhyme. "Though originally a kind of epigrammatic song [a short, poetic observation], passed around orally, *limericks* increased the range of their subject matter to encompass every possible theme, nothing being sacred to their humor. They were chiefly concerned, however, with manners, morals, and peculiarities of imaginary people" (Harmon and Holman 1999: 290).

The limerick is usually written with an anapestic meter (a metrical foot composed of two short syllables and a long one), with a rhyme scheme of A, A, B, B, A. The name *limerick* may have come from an old English custom of singing spontaneous nonsense verses at parties; each performer always closed with a chorus that invited the next performer by saying: Will you come up to limerick? Traditionally, there is a place name in the first line.

Puns

A pun is a play on words based on two similar words that sound much alike but have different meanings. William Shakespeare used puns as wordplay in his dramas. A clear example of a pun is Thomas Hood's: "they went and told the sexton and the sexton tolled the bell" (Harmon and Holman 1999: 418).

Shaggy Dog Story

A shaggy dog story is long and drawn out and often ends rather flatly with a pun. The listener expects a traditional ending to the story, but instead receives a hoax or variation of a familiar saying. The characters and actions are often ridiculous, and the story is told with deliberate elaboration and trivial detail.

Schwank

A schwank is long but straightforward story or narrative that represents tasteless humor and undereducated, often rural characters. The word *schwank* is of German origin, and it is defined as a funny story, joke, or farce. The description of the characters or the unique situation carries the story rather than the punch line at the end.

Sage

Among folklorists, who often have deep roots in European, particularly German, scholarship, the German word *Sage* translates to legend, fable, or myth. The literary folklore scholar Max Lüthi wrote that "Märchen [little story] and Sage [legend] are two basic contingencies of narration" (Lüthi 1961: 7). The Märchen is a fictional fairy tale. Lutz Röhrich states: "The legend [Sage] demands from teller and listener to believe the truth of what it tells" (1958: 664). In other words, like the legend, the Sage is a story that may have some elements of truth.

Spoonerism

The word *spoonerism* comes from the Reverend Doctor William A. Spooner (1844–1930), an English clergyman of New College, Oxford, who became well known for unintentionally changing the sounds of words in his quotations. It refers to humorous word play produced by switching the initial sounds of words as in "Let me sew you to your sheet" for "Let me show you to your seat" (Morris 1982: 1181).

Reports of Reverend Doctor Spooner's difficulty with language may have been exaggerated, but he is said to have told a lazy student, "You've hissed all your mystery lectures and tasted two whole worms" (Harmon and Holman 1999: 492).

Wellerism

Though the concept of a wellerism existed before gaining its name from Charles Dickens's characters Sam and Tony Weller in *Posthumous Papers of the Pickwick Club* (1836, 1837), the form is usually a quotation that has a humorous twist. "The origin and history of wellerisms are quite nebulous. Early examples have been found on Sumerian cuneiform tablets as well as in Classical Greek and Latin Literature" (Meider 1998: 696). Sometimes the wellerism gives a literal interpretation to a figurative comment, such as "the rug said to the floor, 'I've got you covered.'" Or, it might involve a pun, such as "I'm delighted, as the firefly said when he backed into the fan" (Meider and Kingsbury 1994: n.p.).

CLASSIFICATION SYSTEMS

Because of variations in similar folk and fairy tales from region to region, country to country, and throughout the world, scholars recognized that a rigorous and usable classification system needed to be created. Similar stories were being told in places as far apart as Finland and Ceylon. Many explanatory origin theories emerged in attempts to explain why stories with strangely like plots and characters could be surfacing thousands and thousands of miles apart, but the theories faded in time, and the huge task of classification and cross-referencing needed to be accomplished to provide references for scholarly comparative studies.

"In some early studies," Brunvand states, "the numbers of the tales in the Grimm collection [*Kinder- und Hausmärchen,* or *Children's and Household Tales,* 1812] were used for reference purposes. But as large numbers of folktales were collected, serious drawbacks appeared in these systems" (1998:

231). Variations in titles, similar characters, local adaptations, oral tales without titles, and other complexities revealed that the Grimm system of numbering tales was limited only to their collection.

In the middle to late 1800s, scholars in Europe attempted to establish classification systems for both ballads and folktales. Various forms were tried, and in 1910 a Finnish scholar named Antti Aarne produced a catalog named *Verzeichnis der Märchentype*. This began a foundation for a usable classification method, and in 1928, American folklorist Stith Thompson translated and enlarged it (*The Types of the Folktale*) (Brunvand 1998: 231). Thompson revised the index and published it in 1961 as *The Types of the Folktale: A Classification and Bibliography* The Type-Index is usually referred to as the "Aarne-Thompson" or "AT" types by scholars who use and reference it. It combined the systems that Aarne and Thompson developed. In the text *Folkloristics: An Introduction,* Robert Georges and Michael Jones state: "Folklorists use the term *tale type* to identify a group of stories configured into a set and identified in a common way because the similarities discernible in their plots are judged to be too striking and significant quantitatively [in numbers] or qualitatively [having to do with the quality] to be attributed to chance or coincidence" (1995: 24 n.6).

Stith Thompson then continued the classification work and created the *Motif-Index to Folk Literature* (1955–58), a system that classifies international narrative elements such as characters, behaviors, artifacts and objects, settings, and other details. The two systems, the type-index and the motif-index, are cross-referenced, but the first focuses on European tales, while the second is world-ranging and includes motifs or elements from narratives that would not be considered folktales (such as ballads, medieval romances, jestbooks, and other sources of motifs). University libraries have these references, and Thompson's *Motif-Index of Folk-Literature* is available on CD-ROM at: http://www.Indiana.edu/~librcsd/cdrom/Detailed/38.html.

The tale classifications in Thompson's 1961 revision are still used by folklorists throughout the world. There are complementary indices that utilize the Aarne-Thompson system that focus on folktales from non-European countries in Asia and the Americas. Thompson's main classification headings in *The Types of the Folk Tale* are:

I. Animal Tales (1–299)

1–99	Wild Animals
100–149	Wild Animals and Domestic Animals
150–199	Man and Wild Animals
200–219	Domestic Animals

220–249	Birds
250–274	Fish
275–299	Other Animals and Objects

II. Ordinary Folktales (300–1199)

300–749	A. Tales of Magic
300–399	Supernatural Adversaries
400–459	Supernatural or Enchanted Husband (Wife) or Other Relatives
500–559	Supernatural Tasks
560–649	Magic Objects
650–699	Supernatural Power or Knowledge
700–749	Other Tales of the Supernatural
750–849	B. Religious Tales
850–999	C. Novelle (Romantic Tales)
1000–1199	D. Tales of the Stupid Ogre

III. Jokes and Anecdotes (1200–1999)

1200–1349	Numskull Stories
1350–1439	Stories about Married Couples
1440–1524	Stories about a Woman (Girl)
1525–1574	Stories about a Man (Boy)
1575–1639	The Clever Man
1640–1674	Lucky Accidents
1675–1724	The Stupid Man
1725–1849	Jokes about Parsons and Religious Orders
1850–1874	Anecdotes about Other Groups of People
1875–1999	Tales of Lying

IV. Formula Tales (2000–2399)

2000–2199	Cumulative Tales
2200–2249	Catch Tales
2250–2299	Unfinished Tales
2300–2399	Other Formula Tales

V. Unclassified Tales (2400–2499)

| 2400–2499 | Unclassified Tales |

Because the tale-type and motif indices are somewhat complex to use and even occasionally inconsistent in their bibliographical entries, contain a myriad of languages, and often refer to texts that are out of print, more recent scholars have created less complex guidelines for folktale research. Two of these are D. L. Ashliman, who wrote *A Guide to Folktales in the English Language: Based on the Aarne-Thompson Classification System* (1987) and Margaret Read Mac-Donald, who wrote: *The Storyteller's Sourcebook: A Subject, Title, and Motif Index to Folklore Collections for Children* (1982).

The Ashliman text is a useful index of story types that can be expanded and elaborated for storytelling. The MacDonald text is an excellent numerical index to juvenile story publications. MacDonald has adapted the motif-index and provides an index for set stories. Both of these books are for English-speaking scholars and lay researchers. Doug Lipman, a folklore scholar and storyteller, has provided a user-friendly Web site to guide interested researchers in the use of type-indices: http://www.storydynamics.com/Articles/Finding_and_Creating/types.html.

PROPP'S FUNCTIONS

Another perspective on folk and fairy tales useful to scholars, storytellers, and students came from the Russian folklorist Vladimir Propp (1895–1970). In Propp's book, *Morphology of the Folktale* (1968: 25–65), he discussed the structural elements of folktales after analyzing 100 Russian Märchen. His discussion is from what is called Russian Formalism, and the functions he offered as ever-present in Märchen or fairy tales are categorized in scholarly terms as narratology (the study of narrative structure). In the Russian Formalist approach, sentence structures were broken down into elements that could be analyzed. In his approach to folktales, Propp identified narrative structures among them, including the characters and kinds of actions, and concluded that there were 31 generic elements or "narratemes."

He stated that these 31 consistent components or functions work together in pairs in order for the tales to be legitimate or not. He suggested that the functions must unfold in a consistent pattern or order, and that their doing so accounts for the structural stability of the tales. The examples that accompany the list below show how the functions are used as narrative elements in various tales. The 31 functions and contexts he listed are:

Initial Situation: Context

Preparatory Section of the Tale

1. Absence: Someone is missing from the family or social unit.

    Consider a story like "Cinderella." Who is missing? In that story, it is the mother who is missing. In a story like "Sleeping Beauty," who is missing? Certainly in "Sleeping Beauty," the missing person becomes the beautiful princess herself.

2. Interdiction: An instruction of restraint

Think of the instructions to Luke Skywalker in the *Star Wars* film series. In the beginning of the original trilogy, Luke learns about a damsel in distress from R2-D2. R2-D2 draws Luke into the quest, informs him of a damsel in distress, and foreshadows events to come. C-3PO also appears and is soon followed by Obi-Wan (Ben) Kenobi, who gives Luke his history, warnings, and initial instructions.

3. Violation: Violation of some instructions.

At the blessing of the baby princess in "Sleeping Beauty," the parents invited 12 good fairies to bestow the infant with good fortune. They neglected to invite

The uninvited witch pronounced a curse on Sleeping Beauty and her household.

the thirteenth fairy, who arrived and cursed the child with the threat that she would die when she pricked her finger on a spinning wheel. The parents intended to destroy all of the spinning wheels in the kingdom, but overlooked one high in a tower of their castle. The curse, softened by one of the fairies who had not yet given her blessing, was 100 years of sleep for the princess and everyone else in the castle.

4. Reconnaissance: The antihero (villain) seeks information.

In the story of the arrest of Jesus Christ in the Garden of Gethsemane, the anti-heroes are the chief priests and elders of the people led by Judas, the betrayer. They are told that Judas will lead them to the garden and kiss Christ, thereby reveal his identity (Matthew 26). Delilah, loyal to the Philistines, sought to know the source of Samson's strength. Samson believed that his great strength was in his unshorn hair (Judges 13:24–16:30).

5. Delivery: The antihero receives information

Christ was delivered into the hands of his enemies when Judas identified him. (Matthew 26). Samson revealed to Delilah the source of his strength, and she had his head shaved as he slept. The consequence was death to Samson and the Philistines when he managed to pull loose supporting pillars of the building that housed them (Judges 13:24–16:30).

6. Trickery: Deceit by the antihero or antiheroine in order to take possession of the hero or heroine or their possessions.

In the story of *Ali Baba and the Forty Thieves,* Kasim, the greedy brother-in-law of Ali Baba, seeks to learn the magic word (or code) to the treasure cave. He does obtain it, enters the cave, gathers treasures, but fails to remember the word in order to open the cave door to exit. Consequently, he is slain by the robbers when they return to their lair.

7. Complicity: The victim unwittingly submits to deception and helps the anti-hero's goal.

In the story of "Snow White," the poison apple is taken willingly but unknowingly by the victim and causes her to fall into a comalike sleep.

Inauguration of the Plot

8. Villainy: The antihero causes harm to a family member.

The harm may be theft, casting a spell, threats, bodily harm, or other examples of villainy. When the thirteenth witch casts the spell on Aurora, or Sleeping Beauty, or when Snow White falls into the coma after tasting the apple, these actions represent the villain's harmful behavior.

8a. Lack: A member of the family lacks or desires something.

In addition or alternatively to the villainy, there is something missing that needs to be supplied. This often relates to the lack of a bride, groom, or friend. In *Shrek* (both I and II), for instance, Donkey becomes a friend to Shrek, the ogre, and in spite of Shrek's resistance, the friendship satisfies many needs.

9. Mediation: A response by the hero or heroine to a call for help.

At this point, the hero or heroine is appealed to for help. The hero or heroine appears in the story, sometimes for the first time, and the situation is explained to him or her.

10. Beginning counteraction: The hero/heroine agrees to respond.

Sometimes this is not expressed in the story, but it occurs when the hero/heroine overtly responds to the challenge. When the hero is a seeker, as in "Jack and the Beanstalk," the beginning counteraction becomes visible. Jack is pursued by the giant and Jack chops down the beanstalk or ladder to the giant's mansion.

11. Departure: The hero/heroine departs.

In *Star Wars,* Luke must leave his Uncle Owen and Aunt Beru to perform his tasks. Though his aunt and uncle were benign and protective, he must overcome the obstacle of their boundaries and take the first steps of his mission as the hero. He follows R2-D2 into the Dune Sea, and it is there he realizes that he will never really return home again.

12. The first function of the donor or mentor: Testing of the hero/heroine.

In the story of Cupid (Eros) and Psyche, she (our heroine) was warned by Cupid, who loved her deeply, never to look upon him. She was hidden away in an enchanted palace, and he made his visits to her in the night. Cupid was testing the obedience and compliance of Psyche. However, at the suggestion of her jealous sisters, Psyche lit a candle one night and looked upon the handsome, sleeping god. Unfortunately, a drop of wax fell from the candle (or oil from an oil lamp) and awakened him.

13. The hero's/heroine's reaction: reaction to the mentor

In the story of Cupid (Eros) and Psyche, Cupid vanished at the moment of awakening, which left Psyche wandering about for a long time seeking aid from mortals and gods.

14. Provision or receipt of a magical agent: help

The mother of Cupid, or Eros, was the beauty Venus, who was actually jealous of Psyche. Even so, the humble, suffering Psyche appealed to Venus to help her. Psyche was given two seemingly impossible tasks. One was to sort an enormous number of seeds and grain into neat piles, by evening. Ants assisted Psyche, and

Psyche, the beautiful bride of
Eros and daughter-in-law of
the jealous Venus.

the work was accomplished. The second task was to gather some of Proserpine's beauty in a box or urn that Venus provided. In order to obtain it, Psyche had to descend into Hades. She accomplished the task with aid of many kinds, but was curious about the contents of the box, opened it, and immediately fell into a deep sleep because "sleep" is what the box contained (beauty sleep?). Venus took pity on the girl, and the lovers were at last reunited.

15. Guidance: The hero/heroine is transported to the necessary place.

In the wonderful story of "Cinderella," the heroine is transported to the Prince's ball in a pumpkin, which has been changed, magically, into a carriage. The Disney studio's *Cinderella* created colorful visual animation to let viewers see the process through which animals are changed into driver, horses, and coachmen. In fairy tales, heroes and heroines are transported by magic carpets, underwater crafts, and time machines, always arriving where they need to be just in the nick of time.

Struggle with Villain and Villainy

16. Struggle: Combat between the hero/heroine and antihero.

In the story of *Sir Gawain and the Green Knight,* the two title characters ultimately meet at Green Castle for the culmination of the headless Green Knight's challenge a year earlier. The face-to-face "battle" turns out to be one of words, rather than swords, and Sir Gawain, who has been sorely tested by the wife of Bertilak (the Green Knight), feels that he has failed. Though he did not yield to her physical temptations, he did accept a green scarf or sash from her and attempted to keep that hidden from Bertilak. The word *battle* turns out to be somewhat playful, both mocking and praising, and Gawain feels he has lost the encounter because he failed to remain open and honest about his choice of accepting the scarf.

17. Branding, marking: A wound, sign, or object used for identification.

One of the most famous uses for an identity is in the Old Testament of the Bible. Because of the surmised oral nature of many of these ancient stories, many scholars consider them to be folktales. In Genesis 4:15, Cain was punished for killing his brother. The scripture states: "And the Lord said unto him, Therefore whosoever slayeth Cain, vengeance shall be taken on him sevenfold. And the Lord set a mark upon Cain, lest any finding him should kill him" (Gen. 4:15).

18. Victory: The antihero is defeated.

The story of Aladdin, or Ala-ed-Din, as it is sometimes spelled, has several versions. In a text called *Stories from a Thousand and One Nights,* published between 1909 and 1914, the villains, a Moorish sorcerer and his accursed brother, were both killed by the hero Aladdin. The first died by poison, and the second was stabbed to death (Eliot, Lane, and Lane-Poole: 2001, n.p.).

19. (No designator): The misfortune is eliminated.

Again, referring to Aladdin and his magic lamp, the misfortune of the lamp being in the hands of the enemy is resolved when, after murdering the villain, Aladdin recaptures the lamp.

20. Return: The hero/heroine returns to their beginning location (home).

Aladdin's bride, the princess, is transported (along with their abode) to Africa, far away from their homeland in China, by the evil sorcerer. After the sorcerer and

Aladdin, the lamp, and the peculiar but powerful Genie of the lamp.

his brother are destroyed, Aladdin and his princess (and their castle) are transported back to the city of their birth in China.

21. Pursuit/Chase: The hero/heroine is pursued and threatened.

In the story of "Little Red Riding Hood," the big, mean wolf certainly pursues
the maiden. Many other stories reflect the pursuit of the good hero or heroine by
an evil adversary.

22. Rescue: Rescue of the hero/heroine from pursuit.

Using the example of "Little Red Riding Hood," in most versions, the woodsman
rescues both the child heroine and her grandmother from certain death by the wolf.

23. Unrecognized arrival: The hero/heroine is not recognized at home.

In the tale of "Cinderella," Cinderella is not recognized as the princess at the ball by her sisters or stepmother.

24. Unfounded Claims: False hero/heroine presents unfounded claims.

Again in "Cinderella," the stepsisters deceitfully present themselves as the princess to those who are searching for the owner of the lost slipper. In some versions of the story, the two sisters cut their heel or toe in order to make their foot slip into the tiny slipper.

Task and Solution

25. Difficult Task: Hero/heroine must pass an ordeal or test.

In many stories, including Psyche and Cupid (Eros) and some versions of "Cinderella," the heroine is required to meet seemingly impossible demands such as picking up thousands of pieces of grain or lentils, or spinning huge amounts of straw into gold overnight.

26. Solution: The task is resolved.

In many tales, birds, insects, or ants assist in accomplishing the heroine's task.

27. Recognition: The brand or sign of the hero/heroine is recognized.

In "Cinderella," the heroine is identified when her foot slips easily into the glass slipper.

28. Exposure: The antihero is found out.

In some of the more grisly versions of "Cinderella," the evil stepsisters are identified and blinded permanently by birds.

29. Transfiguration: The hero/heroine is given a new appearance.

The delightful transfiguration of Cinderella from a dirty scullery maiden to a richly attired princess is no more clearly presented than in Walt Disney's animated film *Cinderella*.

30. Punishment: The antihero is punished, banished, tortured, killed.

Recalling the stories of Aladdin and his magic lamp, the sorcerer and his evil brother are both put to painful death by poison and stabbing. In one version (James Kunstler's *Aladdin and the Magic Lamp*), the villain is put to death by the bite of a deadly viper. As he dies, the description states: "The magician's eyes crossed, smoke curled out his narrow nostrils, and his thin lips babbled wordlessly until he keeled over as dead as a stone" (Kunstler 1995: 30).

31. Wedding: The hero/heroine is married and ascends a throne.

From "Cinderella" to "Sleeping Beauty," many folk and fairy tales end with the proverbial "Happy ever after," as the happily joined hero and heroine marry and ascend the throne to love and reign, more or less, forever.

Propp's study helped him to identify types of tales, but he also wanted to determine, as much as he was able, which parts of the fairy tales were absolutely necessary for the success of the tale. Eva Thury and Margaret Devinney wrote that a scholar named A. J. Greimas generalized Propp's system of classification and reduced the 31 functions to a system or pattern called "The Quest." This "consists of a qualifying test, a main test, and a glorifying test, and the consequence of each" (Thury and Devinney 2005: 520). Propp's functions have been challenged by other scholars over time, in part because he did not discuss the diverse and important aspects of the tales' social functions.

The next chapter is a sampling of stories from around the world, and within the stories are many examples of the types of prose narratives described in the last several pages. These are narratives that have lasted over time because people have found in them familiar themes and meaningful information. About half of the following tales have originated in the English-speaking world, and the other half are from the non-English-speaking world. From traditional European fairy tales to contemporary American revisions of fairy tales, from ballads to fables, and from jokes to humorous anecdotes, these are a sampling of stories that are shared in families, schools, professional storytelling gatherings, and in other places around our storytelling world.

WORKS CITED

Abrahams, Rogers D. 1968. "Trickster, the Outrageous Hero." In *Our Living Traditions: An Introduction to American Folklore,* ed. Tristram P. Coffin, 170–78. New York: Basic Books.

Adams, Linda Kinsey. 1990. "Folk Narrative." In *The Emergence of Folklore in Everyday Life,* ed. George H. Schoemaker. Bloomington, IN: Trickster Press.

Aesop. 1998. *The Fables of Aesop.* London: The Folio Society.

Ashliman, D. L. 1987. *A Guide to Folktales in the English Language: Based on the Aarne-Thompson Classification System.* Westport, CT: Greenwood Press.

Bascom, William. 1954. "Four Functions of Folklore." *Journal of American Folklore* 67: 333–49.

———. 1965. "The Forms of Folklore: Prose Narratives." *Journal of American Folklore* 78: 3–20.

Beidelman, T. O. 1993. "The Moral Imagination of the Kaguru: Some Thoughts on Tricksters, Translation, and Comparative Analysis." In *Mythical Trickster*

Figures: Contours, Contexts, and Criticisms, ed. William J. Hynes and William G. Doty, 174–92. Tuscaloosa: University of Alabama Press.

Bishop, Holley. 2005. *Robbing the Bees: A Biography of Honey.* New York: Free Press.

Botkin, B. A. [1944] 1989. *The Treasury of American Folklore: Stories, Ballads, and Traditions of the People.* New York: American Legacy Press.

Bronner, Simon J. 1998. *Following Tradition: Folklore in the Discourse of American Culture.* Logan: Utah State University Press, 1998.

Brunvand, Jan Harold. 1986. *The Study of American Folklore: An Introduction.* New York: W.W. Norton and Company.

———. 1998. *The Study of American Folklore: An Introduction.* 4th ed. New York: W. W. Norton.

Dégh, Linda. 1995. *Narratives in Society: A Performer-Centered Study of Narration.* Helsinki: Academia Scientiarum Fennica.

Dolby, Sandra. 1977. "The Oral Personal Narrative in Its Generic Context." *Fabula* 18: 18–39.

———. 1989. *Literary Folkloristics and the Personal Narrative.* Bloomington: Indiana University Press.

Dundes, Alan. 1989. *Folklore Matters.* Knoxville: University of Tennessee Press.

Eliade, Mircea. 1975. *Myth and Reality.* New York: Harper Colophon.

Eliot, Charles William, Edward William Lane, and Stanley Lane-Poole. [1909–14] 2001. *Stories from the Thousand and One Nights.* The Harvard Classics, vol. 16. New York: P. F. Collier and Son. Available at http://www.bartleby.com/16/, posted 2001. Accessed 14 September 2005.

"Frequently Asked Questions (and Answers) about Fan Fiction." Available at: http:// chillingeffects.org/fanfic/jaq.cgi). Accessed 3 July 2005.

Freytag, Gustav. [1863] 1904. *Freytag's Technique of Drama.* North Stratford, NH: Ayer Company.

Fulford, Robert. 1999. *The Triumph of Narrative: Storytelling in the Age of Mass Culture.* Toronto: Anansi Press.

Georges, Robert A., and Michael Owen Jones. 1995. *Folkloristics: An Introduction.* Bloomington: Indiana University Press.

Hallett, Martin, and Barbara Karasek. 1996. *Folk and Fairy Tales.* 2d ed. Peterborough, Ontario: Broadview Press.

Harmon, William, and C. Hugh Holman. 1999. *A Handbook to Literature.* 8th ed. Upper Saddle River, NJ: Prentice Hall.

Harry Potter Fan Fiction Web site. http://harrypotterfanfiction.com/. Last accessed 3 July 2005.

Hoever, Hugo. 1989. *Lives of the Saints for Every Day of the Year.* New York: Catholic Book Publishing.

Holzberg, Niklas. 2002. *The Ancient Fable: An Introduction.* Bloomington: Indiana University Press.

Hornstein, Lillian Herlands, Leon Edel, and Horst Frenz, eds. 1973. *The Readers Companion to World Literature.* New York: A Mentor Book/New American.

Jacobs, Joseph, ed. [1894] 1966. *The Fables of Aesop*. New York: Schocken Books/ Pantheon Books/Random House.

Kunstler, James Howard. 1995. *Aladdin and the Magic Lamp*. New York: Simon and Schuster.

Kurlansky, Mark. 2005. *Salt: A World History*. New York: Penguin Books.

Lee, Terry. 2003. "Journalist, Teacher, and Storyteller." *Points of Entry: Cross-Currents in Storytelling* 1 (1): 7–12.

Lindahl, Carl, John McNamara, and John Lindow, eds.. 2002. *Medieval Folklore: A Guide to Myths, Legends, Tales, Beliefs, and Customs*. New York: Oxford University Press.

Lipman, Doug. "In Search of the Folktale." Available at: http:www.storydynamics. com/Articles/Finding_and_Creating/types.html.Accessed 20 July 2005. An earlier version of this article appeared in *The Yarnspinner,* 2005.

Lüthi, Max. 1961. *Volksmärchen und Volkssage,* zwei Grundformen erzählender Dichtung. Bern: Francke.

———. 1976. *Once upon a Time: On the Nature of Fairy Tales*. Bloomington: Indiana University Press.

MacDonald, Margaret Read. 1982. *The Storyteller's Sourcebook: A Subject, Title, and Motif Index to Folklore Collections for Children*. 1st ed. Detroit: Gale Research.

Maier, John. 2002. "Gilgamesh." In *The Epic Voice,* ed. Alan D. Hodder and Robert E. Meagher, 15–51. Hampshire Studies in the Humanities. Westport, CT: Praeger Publishers.

Medsger, Betty. 1996. *Winds of Change: Challenges Confronting Journalism Education*. Arlington, VA: The Freedom Forum.

Meider, Wolfgang. 1998. "Wellerisms." In *Encyclopedia of Folklore and Literature,* ed. Mary Ellen Brown and Bruce A. Rosenberg, 695–96. Santa Barbara, CA: ABC-CLIO.

Meider, Wolfgang, and Stewart A. Kingsbury. 1994. *A Dictionary of Wellerisms*. New York: Oxford University Press.

Miller, Carolyn Handler. 2004. *Digital Storytelling: A Creator's Guide to Interactive Entertainment*. New York: Focal Press.

Morris, William. 1982. *The American Heritage Dictionary,* Second College Edition. Boston, MA: Houghton Mifflin.

Polley, Jane, ed. 1978. *American Folklore and Legend*. Pleasantville, NY: Reader's Digest.

Propp, Vladimir. 1928/1968. *Morphology of the Folktale,* 2nd ed., trans. Laurence Scott, rev. and ed. by Louis A. Wagner. Publications of the American Folklore Society, Bibliographical and Special Series 9. Austin: University of Texas Press.

Radin, Paul. 1972. *The Trickster: A Study in American Indian Mythology*. New York: Schocken Books.

Röhrich, Lutz. 1958. *Die Deutsche Volkssage. Studium Generale* 11:664–91.

Simonsen, Michéle. 2002. "Animal Tale." In *Medieval Folklore: A Guide to Myths, Legends, Tales, Beliefs, and Customs,* ed. Carl Lindahl, John McNamara, and John Lindow, 13–16. New York: Oxford University Press.

Stern, James, ed. 1972. *The Complete Grimm's Fairy Tales.* New York: Pantheon Books.

Tangherlini, Timothy R. 2002. "Legend." In *Medieval Folkore: A Guide to Myths, Legends, Tales, Beliefs, and Customs,* ed. Carl Lindahl, John McNamara, and John Lindow, 240–43. New York: Oxford University Press.

Taylor, Archer. 1985. *The Proverb and an Index to "The Proverb."* New York: Peter Lang.

Thomas, Gerald. 1996. "Tall Tale." In *American Folklore: An Encyclopedia,* ed. Jan Harold Brunvand, 700–702. New York: Garland.

Thompson, Stith. 1961. *The Types of the Folktale: A Classification and Bibliography.* 2d. rev. ed. Folklore Fellows Communication 184 (Helsinki). CD-ROM available at: http://www.indiana.edu/~librcsd/cdrom/Detailed/38.html. Accessed 8 August 2005.

Thury, Eva M., and Margaret K. Devinney. 2005. *Introduction to Mythology: Contemporary Approaches to Classical and World Myths.* New York/Oxford: Oxford University Press.

Toelken, Barre. 1995. *Morning Dew and Roses: Nuance, Metaphor, and Meanings in Folksongs.* Urbana: University of Illinois Press.

Tucker, Elizabeth. 1998. "Nursery Rhymes." In *Encyclopedia of Folklore and Literature,* ed. Mary Ellen Brown and Bruce A. Rosenberg, 458–60. Santa Barbara: CA: ABC-CLIO.

Weems, Mason L. 1809/1976. *The Life of Washington,* ed. Marcus Cunliffe. Cambridge: Belknap Press.

Three
Examples and Texts

The last chapter began with a discussion of what a story is. As stated there, a good story makes us want to know what is going to happen next. When you apply some of the elements of story discussed there to a simple tale like "Little Red Riding Hood," the parts of the story are easy to identify. Aristotle and scholars after him taught that each story must have a plot, setting, characters, theme, rising actions, conflict, and resolution. In the story of "Little Red Riding Hood," we know that the basic plot has everything to do with danger for our primary character, or *protagonist,* who is an unprotected child. The other primary character, the *antagonist* in this story, is a terrifying wolf. The setting is the forest—a dark, mysterious, unpredictable place. An analytical examination of this story and its folkloric theme and elements suggests that the child represents innocence, the forest represents mystery and hidden threats, and the wolf, physical danger. These can be interpreted to be symbolic of the dangers involved in passing from the innocence of childhood to an informed state of adult life. Though no one knows the origin of this tale, the underlying conflict is transition or change. The resolution is provided by a minor character, the rescuing woodsman, and ultimately Red Riding Hood and her grandmother (another minor character) are united in peace and safety.

In Freytag's pyramid, the beginning explanation or exposition sets the story up for the reader or hearer. The characters, setting, and circumstances (entering the forest to deliver a treat to the grandmother) are put forward to begin the story. Then, the story becomes more complicated as Red Riding Hood passes into the danger of the forest. In some stories, the wolf is described as lurking about, watching the child as she merrily passes through the woods quite unaware of impending danger. This is tension building, and Freytag labeled this part of a story "rising action." The wolf determines the goal of Red Riding Hood and races ahead to the grandmother's house, swallows her in a gulp, and then dons her nightgown and cap. When Red Riding Hood arrives at the bedside, she notes that her grandmother looks quite extraordinary, and launches into the familiar litany, "Oh Grandmother, what big eyes . . . what a big nose . . . what big teeth you have!"

To which the wolf replies, "The better to see, to smell, to eat you with," and lunges at the child. This exchange is the climax of the story, and after the wolf swallows our brave little heroine, the woodsman provides the turning point and resolution of the story. He somehow hears or senses that something is wrong, breaks into the house, slays the wolf, and Grandmother and Red Riding Hood are saved to live happily ever after (the denouement or outcome). These elements of story are traditionally present, but there are stories that do not quite unravel or clarify.

Little Red Riding Hood and the Big, Bad Wolf. *The Granger Collection, New York.*

WRITTEN LITERATURE

Most written literature contains elements of folklore. It would be nearly impossible to write either fiction or nonfiction and not include motifs that represent what people say, make, do, and believe. History texts, from antiquity to contemporary products, unconsciously represent the time in which they are written. That is, they reflect points of view, cultural practices, artifacts, and language that portrays the practices of the day. Mythology, legends, folktales, and fiction all incorporate the basic elements of folklore. Though authors create original plots, settings, themes, and characters, still present are traditional behaviors and folkways of the people in the stories.

Reaching far back into time and space and retrieving one of the wonderful stories that Publius Ovidius Naso (better known to us as Ovid) wrote in Rome in the days of Augustus, we find traditional behavior reflected in the denouement of the tender story of Narcissus, a beautiful boy, and Echo, a nymph, who, when spurned by the boy, wasted away to nothing but a voice. Theirs was a story of pride, vanity, and frustration, and in the end, a story of simple consequence. Narcissus so admired his own beauty in reflected pools, that he fell in love with himself. Frustrated with not being able to grasp his image, he mourned and called out, "Alas."

Echo responded with "Alas," and then he cried, "Farewell."

Again, Echo replied, "Farewell."

Beating himself to death, "His weary head sank to the grass; death closed those eyes transfixed once by their master's beauty, but on the ferry ride across the Styx [the river to Hades] his gaze into its current did not waver" (Martin 2005: 110). The story closes with these lines reflecting the customary, folkloric tradition:

> The water nymphs, his sisters, cut their locks
> in mourning for him, and the wood nymphs too,
> And Echo echoed all their lamentations;
> but after they'd arranged his funeral
> gotten the logs, the bier, the brandished torches,
> The boy's remains were nowhere to be found;
> instead, a flower, whose white petals fit
> closely around a saffron-colored center.
> (2005: 110, 111)

The evidence of customary, folkloric behavior is represented by "the logs, the bier, the brandished torches," all typical elements of funerary practice in the time of Ovid. From the ancient writings of India's *Ramayana* to *Huckleberry Finn* (1884), to the contemporary popular fiction of *Harry Potter* and even the author Dan Brown's creative *The Da Vinci Code* (2003), we see evidence of folklore in the stories again and again.

Literature for Entertainment

Though literature is often used to teach principles and behavior from generation to generation, it is most often created to entertain. From complex ancient epics like *Gilgamesh,* whose title character quests for immortality, to contemporary entertainment like T. A. Barron's novels about the Arthurian character of Merlin *(The Lost Years of Merlin, The Seven Songs of Merlin, The Fires of Merlin),* writers write, publishers publish, and readers read. Readers are captured and carried away in mythic imaginations by paragraphs like this one from *The Seven Songs of Merlin:*

> But it was too late. My mother stumbled, rolling down the dune. When she stopped, I saw that her entire face was covered by a writhing shadow. Then, to my horror, the shadow slithered into her mouth and disappeared. (Barron 2001: 82)

The creepy feeling one experiences when reading such a passage as this is created by the skillful use of folklore. Most humans have a reasonable respect for snakes for good reason. Many snakes are deadly, and the snake has been used as a symbol for evil since antiquity. There are many superstitions attached to snakes. Edward Dolan, in a text called *Animal Folklore: From Black Cats to White Horses* (1992), wrote:

> If your are a product of the American south, especially Kentucky, the chances are that you early learned to be upset by dreams of a snake, for it means the bad luck of having enemies somewhere close by. But if you then dream of killing the snake, you should feel much relieved. It indicates that you have bested and defeated your adversaries. However, if the snake escapes, you are to be wary of others and take great care in your dealings with them. (63)

These are superstitions, of course, but they permeate our contemporary culture, and creative writers draw from the feelings they evoke to provoke and entertain us. Many readers enjoy the tension that suspenseful passages such as Barron's trigger, and that is part of literature's role. We read fictional stories for many reasons, and the primary ones are to be transported to another time and place and to be entertained.

Literature for Didactic (or Teaching) Purposes

Human attitudes and cultural behaviors can be shaped by literature. Through the use of riddles, proverbs, and parables, as well as anecdotal stories and allegory (stories that have more than one meaning), parents, teachers, and priests and ministers aid both themselves and others in learning appropriate social conduct. The responsibility of transmitting information and helping others to an understanding of social and moral behavior is a vital one in ongoing society, and specifically didactic literature is one means by which this can be accomplished.

For more than two and a half centuries, the Hasidic Jews have practiced a rich, oral culture. Founded by the Baal Shem Tov (1700–60) in Eastern Europe, the tradition followed his example of using tales, parables, and legends to educate and train his people. Many hasidim have migrated to the United States and the men can be identified by their long black jackets, black hats, distinctive beards, and often long, curled sideburns. The women wear wigs in public, and they usually dress simply. The children dress much like their elders, though most of the girls wear long braids.

The rebbe (rabbi) in this tradition continues to use stories to teach the people proper attitudes and behaviors, and parents in this tradition use stories to help train and transmit the culture to their children. "Storytelling won an established place in the life of the earliest hasidim and it became part of the Shabbes [Sabbath] ritual. On the Shabbes, the men met three times to pray and to share communal meals . . . the Rebbes [who were present] often wove their teachings into an extended metaphor or parable or told an illustrative tale" (Mintz 1968: 4). Many of these stories have been recorded in writing, and they are now available to the reading public in the form of literary legends and stories of the mystic, hasidim culture. What was once oral tradition has become a written literature.

The following story called, "The Silver Casket (H15)," was told for the purpose of teaching people not to steal, because thieves are usually found out.

In Annopol, in the Ukaraine, a casket of silver was stolen from the king. He naturally accused the Jews and threatened them with expulsion. So they went to Reb Zusya of Annopol, the brother of Rebbe Elimelekh, and he told them to tell the king that in three to four months he guarantees that he will have the money back.

The time came closer and closer and he did not bother to raise the necessary money. So finally when it was only a few days before the end of the term, he sent a message to the king that he is coming, and he wants the king to greet him with all his army and servants lined up.

The king complied and he came to greet Reb Zusya. Reb Zusya came and looked over the army and he said, "Someone is missing. The garbage collector is missing." So they found him and put him in line. And Reb Zusya said in a sentence from the prayers of Rosh Hashoneh. The sentence is: "We are asking God to spread His fear throughout the world. Make the world fear You."

The garbage collector hear this and started screaming, "Please don't repeat that again. If you do I'll drop dead." And he immediately confessed and showed the king that he had stolen the silver and he had placed it in the garbage barrel so that no one could find it and he could take it later. (241)

Another story, told to raise the people's faith and belief in the wisdom of the rebbe, is called *The Second Child* (H84).

My grandfather tells me that when my mother became pregnant, when it came close to the ninth month, grandfather took father and went to the Belzer Rebbe. It was close to the time, and is was customary that the Belzer should give a blessing. My grandfather told him of the circumstances, but the Belzer did not answer. He repeated it twice, "I want a blessing." The Rebbe said something, but he just mumbled. The child died. When my mother became pregnant the second time my grandfather and father went again. This time when they told the Rebbe he took a terrific interest, told them which hospital to go to, which doctor to take, to go at a certain time, and he assured them everything will be perfect. To them it was a miracle. It was a sign that he saw that the first child would not live and he did not want to say good luck, to give his blessing. (300)

Much of the literature written today *was* traditional lore; that is, for centuries it was not written and was passed from generation to generation by tellers. In the last century and a half, many of the world's traditional stories have been recorded and then transcribed into written stories or literature. Though many traditional stories exist that are still not collected or written down by folklorists, anthropologists, and other fieldworkers, many have been, and they are now included in the collections of world didactic literature.

Journalism

Since the days when the Greek and Roman empires were at their peak, reports have been made about vast monsters from the dark, hiding places of the sea. Giant squid are pictured on a prized early (sixth century B.C.E.) Corinthian vase housed in Boston's Museum of Fine Arts. While studying fossils from the coast of Troy, Adrienne Mayor, a classical folklorist, began to connect the idea that some of the ancient depictions and stories of giants, heroes, and monsters may have been inspired by a core of truth about what may have been observed washed up on beaches centuries before the birth of Christ. Mayor subsequently published a study about the possibility of legends and myths based on exaggerated or fantasized elements of reality that the early Greeks and Romans observed. Speaking of the mysterious *Architeuthis*—giant squid—Mayor wrote, "This stupendous monster, said to grow to at least 60 feet (18 m) long, with lidless eyes the size of dinner plates, has long inspired terror and awe, as storytellers (most famously Jules Verne), artists, and zoologists try to visualize its appearance and behavior" (Mayor 2000: 230).

In September 2005, journalists from around the world reported that the first photographs of a live, deep-sea squid *(Architeuthis)* had been released by Japanese scientists. The animal, which appears to be approximately 25 feet long, was photographed at nearly 3,000 feet beneath the North Pacific Ocean. As James Owen, a writer for *National Geographic News,* reported,

> Like something straight out of a Jules Verne novel, an enormous tentacled creature looms out of the inky blackness of the deep Pacific waters. . . . the squid was found feeding at depths where no light penetrates even during the day. . . . The mysterious creature has inspired countless sea monster tales and has been the subject of various scientific expeditions. (Owen 2005: 1)

Terry Lee reminded us in the discussion of journalism in chapter 2 that journalists participate in the "business of making meaning, and [assist us] to learn something about the business of being human" (2003: 8). Journalistic narratives like the September 2005 breaking news of not only discovery but photographs of a living giant squid assist us to close or at least add to long-standing narrative gaps. Ancient inhabitants of the world explained various mysteries of nature they observed through creative stories and lore. That lore became the mythology, legends, and folktales that ultimately emerged as the classic literature we read in our contemporary world.

The journalists, excited to sell their work, have written the accounts of this marvelous living, giant squid discovery as creatively as the ancient tales of old by making allusions to tales written about previously unconfirmed leviathans in our placid-looking oceans. With careful description, specificity of detail, and expressed excitement, the journalists have built tension and excitement into their stories by including statements reflecting the delight of the scientists, for instance, "'I think it's wonderful that we've finally got a picture of a living giant squid,' said Richard Ellis, a research associate of the American Museum of Natural History in New York and author of *The Search for the*

Giant Squid" (Owen 2005: 2). By creative storytelling, the journalists draw us into the circle of discovery and discussion and help us with an exciting narrative of many dimensions and kaleidoscopic meaning.

Historical Literature

In the earlier discussion of historical literature, it was mentioned that settings, factual characters, and places can all be invented. One of the most famous American historical stories to be written and greatly distorted is the childhood narrative of George Washington, first president of the United States. In a biography of mostly historical fiction, Mason L. Weems created a credible fiction that has become familiar folklore in our American cultural knowledge is sometimes called cultural capital (meaning items that informed, cultural awareness include), and it is important because it helps us to uderstand and function successfully in society. The cherry tree story is part of American lore and mythic honor, and many Americans know the tale.

Mason L. Weems: George Washington and the Cherry Tree

The story, commonly passed along as a valid myth in our American schools for over 200 years, is that of George Washington and the cherry tree. George's often quoted line, "I can't tell a lie, Pa; you know I can't tell a lie. I did cut it with my hatchet" (Weems 1976: 12) is part of a fictionalized biography of George Washington written by Parson Mason L. Weems in 1800, only a few months after Washington's death, December 14, 1799.

After the death of Washington there were many sermons and memorial tributes made by clergymen in the United States. Weems, who had already published several biographical editions on various American leaders (Benjamin Franklin, William Penn, and others), seized the opportunity and put together a pamphlet about Washington. Over time, the pamphlet went through several editions, and it grew from a few pages to a text of over 200 pages. He promoted himself as a former rector of Mount Vernon Parish, and though he was an ordained Episcopalian minister, there is no documentation that he was actually a rector at Mount Vernon. The following is Weems's version of the cherry tree story from *The Life of Washington* by Mason L. Weems, edited by Marcus Cunliffe. Weems claimed to have obtained the rudiments of this story from a distant relative of Washington's.

> When George . . . was about six years old, he was made the wealthy master of a *hatchet!* Of which, like most little boys, he was immoderately fond, and

Did George Washington cut down his father's cherry tree, or not? *The Granger Collection, New York.*

was constantly going about chopping every thing that came in his way. One day, in the garden, where he often amused himself hacking his mother's pea sticks, he unluckily tried the edge of his hatchet on the body of a beautiful young English cherry-tree, which he barked so terribly, that I don't believe the tree got the better of it. The next morning the old gentleman finding out what had befallen his tree, which, by the by, was a great favorite, came into the house and with much warmth asked for the mischievous author, declaring at the same time, that he would not have taken five guineas for his tree. Nobody could tell him anything about it. Presently George and his hatchet made their appearance. *George,* said his father, *do you know who killed that beautiful little cherry-tree yonder in the garden?* This was a *tough question;* and George staggered under it for a moment; but quickly recovered himself: and looking at his father, with the sweet face of youth brightened with the inexpressible charm of all-conquering truth, he bravely cried out, *I can't tell a lie, Pa; you know I can't tell a lie. I did cut it with my hatchet.—Run to my arms, you dearest boy,* cried his father in transports, *run to my arms; glad am I, George, that you killed my tree; for you have paid me for it a thousand fold. Such an act of heroism in my son, is more worth than a thousand trees, though blossomed with silver, and their fruits of purest gold.* (Weems 1809/1976: 12)

And so, historical literature can sometimes join the mainstream history as a factual representation of past events. In this instance, the story is false, but nevertheless, it is passed along as a tribute to the honesty of the first American president.

Digital Storytelling

Digital storytelling has become a modern technological expression of the ancient art of storytelling. Leslie Rule, of the Digital Storytelling Association, states that, "Digital stories derive their power by weaving images, music, narrative and voice together, thereby giving deep dimension and vivid color to characters, situations, experiences, and insights" (Rule 2005: 1). The method is popular in education, families, and business, and it has become an international Internet storytelling location. Participants have a professional association (the Digital Storytelling Association) as well as national and international conferences and yearly festivals ongoing since 1995.

Quoting an anonymous explanation on the home page of the DigiTales Web site, , "Digital storytelling begins with the notion that in the not distant future, sharing one's story through the multiple mediums of digital imagery, text, voice, sound, music, video and animation will be the principal hobby of the world's people." Because of the relatively easy access to the Internet throughout much of the world, this is a growing venue for biography and histories, both personal and historical. The Digital Storytelling Web site (see http://electronicportfolios.com/digistory) is a repository of many links to other Internet sites that share information about digital storytelling. Surfing that site revealed stories that included narratives from Holocaust survivors, Japanese American internees, and World War II camp liberators.

A text posted at the Digital Storytelling Association Web site employed a metaphoric format to encourage participants to use story to make an impact and difference in one another's lives. Brenda Laurel's "A Tale About Some Crows" reminds us that "storytelling is a relationship . . . and relationships are interactive". Laurel reminds her readers that "The Celtic bards in their crow-feathered robes were the storytellers and lawgivers and news reporters of their day," and then she suggests that a group of contemporary crows were sitting on a wire having a talk. They were preening their feathers and exchanging reliable tales that they had gathered from near and far, when they spied a machine below them that could be used to transport their stories all over the world. Technology, of course, and the text continues, "that is why stories fall like tiny gems from all our beaks . . . through those wires under our little crow feet . . . and between our feathers when we fly" (Laurel: n.p.).

Digital storytelling has become a valuable resource for interactive story sharing and is evidence of the evolutionary patterns in the way stories are told. Long ago, stories were told orally, and sometimes visual illustrations were found on the walls of caves or bluffs. Stories were told around campfires and on trails. Over time, scrolls and books came into being, and in the past few decades, films, videos, and DVDs carry many of the stories of our culture. Now, digital storytelling has found a home on the computer screen, and those stories are widely available to international Internet users.

Fan Fiction

As noted in chapter 2, fan fiction (or FanFic) is another phenomenon of technology. It is writing on the Internet that responds to and adds to popular fiction. Writers can enter fan fiction Web sites covering a broad range, from classics to popular fiction, and from anime (Japanese animation) to TV shows, and create their own versions of existing narratives using artistic license.

Though there are many sites on the Internet for devoted to specific FanFic, the fanfiction.net site offers a vast compilation of hundreds of titles, and the interested user can click on any one of them and read variants created by amateur writers (see http://www.fanfiction.net). Clicking on writings pertaining to *To Kill a Mockingbird* by Harper Lee, I found a poem called "Mockingbird" by Nigeline. Nigeline begins with a disclaimer: "I do not own the most wonderful work of *To Kill a Mockingbird*. That belongs to Harper Lee." Yet Nigeline, the almost anonymous writer, has captured some of the poignant meanings in the text while creating a poem for a creative writing contest in an English class. Her poem can be found at the *To Kill a Mockingbird* FanFic site. See if you can find it.

MYTHS WRITTEN IN ENGLISH

The last several pages of this chapter have described stories in written form. The next pages contextualize and describe different types of orally transmitted stories. Though many of these stories are written, these myths, legends, and the featured folktale have been circulated in verbal form over time by many people of many ages throughout the United States. These are often read or told in elementary schools, and the stories become part of traditional American enculturation or socialization; that is, part of the basic national tapestry of ideas and cultural knowledge. The stories presented in this section— the North American Thanksgiving myth, the legend of Johnny Appleseed plus a couple of urban legends, and the Brer Rabbit folktales, as written by

The first American Thanksgiving menu included venison and other foods. *Library of Congress.*

Joel Chandler Harris—have become well known through both written and oral lore in the United States for many good reasons.

Thanksgiving has become the most widely celebrated holiday in the United States. It has become almost a civic responsibility to honor that holiday with family and friends or to participate in communal celebrations if that presents itself as an opportunity. The first Thanksgiving was celebrated in the harvest time of the year, and it may have been connected to earlier, traditional celebrations. As far as we know, it was a sincere and grateful celebration with simple, survival foods. Game and vegetables made up most of the meal, and the food was furnished by pioneers and the American Indians who helped the pioneers survive their first year in the difficult wilderness.

The stories about Johnny Appleseed live in our culture because of the distinctive and ongoing contributions made by this famous eccentric in early America. He not only planted orchards of apple trees in many Eastern states, he also served people by giving warnings of possible attacks he had overheard being planned. He was trusted by both the white colonists and the American Indians, and, as the stories go, his humility and lack of pride endeared him to nearly everyone lucky enough to make his acquaintance.

John Chapman, better known as "Johnny Appleseed." *The Granger Collection, New York.*

Urban legends or urban myths have been recognized as stories that circulate in contemporary society and are often told as true reports. The first one I ever heard was about a girl who died after three or four trips to tanning salons in order to look beautiful in her bridesmaid gown. The rumor was that she had cooker her inner organs and died. There was no truth to it but microwave ovens were new at the time and the story is thought to be evident of the public's fear of new technology. More examples will be shared and discussed in this section.

The folklore narratives of Brer Rabbit and his adventures are narratives with many layers of meaning. Joel Chandler Harris recollected them as tales he had heard on a plantation he lived near when a child. He became a professional journalist and always claimed that he had written and published the delightful Brer Rabbit stories for the pleasure of children. The stories were entertaining, easy to remember, and repeated throughout America by tellers, parents, older siblings, and librarian storytellers. Questions about them continue to tease scholars, critics, and others who would simply like to know more. Were they really metaphorical stories about slaves and slave masters rather than competitive animals? Are the characters in the stories representative of real people? Were the tales really rooted in Africa and carried here? Since it was not uncommon for slaves and American Indians to intermingle, were the tales influenced by American Indian myths and traditions? These are compelling questions, and maybe they will never have clear answers, but regardless, the tales are passed along and remembered by most of the people who grew up in this country.

The North American Thanksgiving Myth

As defined by folklorists, a myth is designated as an origin story, but sometimes what is perceived as an origin story simply turns out to be another kind of a narrative. Myths carry us on journeys into exciting and unknown worlds from other times and places. Sometimes great acts of nations and people are carried through time by myths. Some myths may be false, in that they represent elements that are not scientifically sound or represent characters that never really existed. Sometimes a myth is a collective story; that is, it may be made up of parts of many stories. Even so, myths carry important information about what people have valued and feel is important to transmit from generation to generation over time.

The story of the first Thanksgiving celebration in America has been told over and over again, and the figurative language and visual images used often suggest bountiful tables resplendent with cornucopias and abundant heaps of game, grains, vegetables, and fruits. The reality of that first celebration table may not have been particularly resplendent, but it continues to represent an attitude of thankfulness for survival. The myth, in the sense of untruth, is that it was not the beginning of a traditional and annual harvest celebration that has continued in the United States as the Thanksgiving celebration as we know it today. It was an origin or beginning for the Pilgrims in the colonies. Many had survived an arduous year, and many had died, but Indian tribes throughout the Americas had already traditionally held annual events in the autumn to demonstrate thankfulness to their gods for their food. It was an English tradition to celebrate Michaelmas, traditionally held September 29, which was a simple feast of bread, cheese, and beer. It may have been that the three-day feast was a gift to the settlers from the American Indians, because it is documented that they furnished venison from five deer and several other foods.

The culinary scholar Laura Schenone informs us that by the fall of 1621, at Plymouth, only four of the eighteen married women who came to the Americas on the *Mayflower* were still alive. Elinor Billington, Mary Brewster, Elizabeth Hopkins, and Susanna Winslow probably cooked corn, beans, and squash (nicknamed "three sisters") and took turns supervising the ten surviving children (most of whom were motherless). Five teenage girls and one maidservant also survived, and Schenone informs us that there were fifty-five surviving English colonists, including those mentioned, and about ninety Wampanoag Indians present at the three-day gathering (Schenone 2003: 46).

Sarah Josepha Hale is largely responsible for institutionalizing the Thanksgiving celebrations shared in contemporary U.S. settings today. In 1846, Hale began a 17-year crusade to end the erratic celebration of Thanksgiving. At that time there was no set date, and most of the Southern states did not even know about it. Contacting state governors, various presidents, and secretaries of state, her success was achieved when "In 1863, amidst the Civil War, Lincoln proclaimed a national Thanksgiving Day. He asked for the nation to be thankful for the bounties of nature and to come together, North and South, for a single, unifying day. The holiday that Sarah envisioned became an icon of American life" (119).

One of the discussions folklorists sometimes have with their university students concerns the food served at traditional meals. Some years ago when I was receiving my training, my professor asked us to think about what the Thanksgiving meal would be like if something besides turkey were served. Would it be Thanksgiving if the hostess served trout? Shortly after that, because I had a friend raising pheasants to earn extra cash for the holidays, I purchased several ready-to-cook pheasants from her. I served my family the roasted pheasant accompanied by all the other expected Thanksgiving dishes (mashed potatoes, sweet potatoes, cranberry relish, green beans, rolls, and pumpkin pie). I did not make a turkey because I thought pheasant would be acceptable to them. It wasn't. Though the pheasant was good (and eaten—every bite), the family asked if I would please serve turkey on Thanksgiving thereafter. The professor served his family brown trout that year, but he too said that it would be turkey on the next Thanksgiving holiday. It seems that when our traditional expectations are unmet, it leaves an unsettling feeling that can only be righted by following the custom the next time around.

Legends Written in English

Johnny Appleseed

A legend, as stated earlier, is a story that carries an element of truth. Sometimes the story is entirely true, but most times the story has been passed along and enriched or diminished along the way. The American legends of Johnny Appleseed, whose real name was John Chapman, are rooted in truth, but they have been enhanced. Chapman was a Swedenborgian missionary; he professed a faith that believed in visions and literal visitations from the other side of the grave. To Chapman, stories of angels and spirits were simply true, and in the early 1800s, he regaled American Indians, particularly the Shawnees, with fascinating tales. For nearly 50 years, he roamed Pennsylvania and Indiana planting apple orchards and sharing tales from the other side, and he was sometimes seen as far west as Illinois and Missouri.

It is said that he had little regard for his personal appearance and would barter for clothing with his seeds. Stories abound of his attire, describing him as wearing a tin pan for a hat and coffee sacks with holes cut for his arms and head, as his main body covering. He seldom wore shoes no matter what the weather, and he greatly respected all living things. Stories exist that tell of his interaction with settlers in the Ohio and Missouri regions. In his day, there were still incidents of occasional of Indian aggression. As one legend goes, there was a Frenchman named Bouvet who was living in the Missouri area, and he heard a noise just outside of his door. Upon opening it, there stood a ragtag man, reputed to have been John Chapman himself, who chanted, "I sow while others reap. / Be sure my warning keep. / Indians will come by break of day. / Indians hunting scalps, I say" (Polley 1978:128). This warning saved the settlement, and similar stories about his warnings have been told by people of the time from the region of Mansfield, Ohio, to the Allegheny and Wabash river territory.

Urban Legends

Another kind of legend popular in today's world is called an urban legend or urban myth. These types of stories are circulated among various groups of people, and their origins are often difficult if not impossible to identify. For this reason, urban legends are sometimes labeled as friend-of-a-friend, or FOAF, legends. Sometimes there is a kernel of truth in them, and upon first hearing one it is easy to give the story credibility. Upon closer examination the stories reveal fallacies or conflicted events within them that expose their flaws.

You may have heard stories about white alligators living in the sewers of large cities such as New York or Chicago. Supposedly, those reptiles were purchases as babies in the Southern states by vacationers. Meant to be souvenirs of the trip, the little alligators became too much trouble to care for or began to get bigger than anticipated, and were thus flushed down the toilet into the urban sewer system. Stories circulated about the critters, and there was even a 1980 film by John Sayles, called *Alligators*, but although a February 10, 1935, *New York Times* story reported that an alligator was found in a New York City sewer, no such creatures have been sighted or officially reported since. Jan Brunvand, a folklorist and retired professor, traces the origin of the alligator in the sewer story to the *Times* article and suggests "that there is something unclean and scary hidden underneath the pleasant surface of civilized life" (Thury and Devinney 2005: 5, 6). Brunvand taught that people make up stories to explain away fears they may have. The following story is from his text *Be Afraid, Be Very Afraid: The Book of Scary Urban Legends* (2004). Brunvand collected stories from many sources, and this one came from a collection published by Paul Smith. Brunvand suggested that "This widely told story is usually known as 'The Accidental Cannibals' or 'The Eaten Cremains'" (Brunvand 2004: 101).

Grandmother had gone out to spend Christmas with her cousins who lived in the Far East. She had not seen them for several years and was very excited about the trip. They had always been very kind to her and each Christmas they used to send a present of a jar of special spices to go in the Christmas cake her daughter made.

About two weeks before Christmas, a small airmail parcel arrived from the Far East. It had been posted on 1 December and contained what appeared to be the special spices for the Christmas cake. There was no note with it nor, surprisingly, any Christmas card. Not wanting to delay any longer, the daughter got on with the baking and produced a magnificent cake for the Christmas festivities.

It was the day after Boxing Day [December 26] that a letter arrived from the cousins in the Far East. Also dated 1 December, it expressed how sorry they were to have to break the news of grandmother's death–the excitements had been too much for her. They also wrote that, because of all the arrangements that had to be made for the cremation, they would not have time to send over the special spices for the cake this year. However, they had airmailed grandmother's ashes home and they should arrive shortly. (Smith 1983: 106)

Brunvand also wrote by way of explanation: "Urban legends are packed with local details and related with an air of conviction. While these stories are not literally true, any more than a horror film is, when hearing them we realize that they *could* be true!" (Brunvand 2004: 13).

A Folktale Written in English

In the late 1900s, Joel Chandler Harris published many tales he had heard as a child. Growing up in Georgia before and during the Civil War, he often visited a nearby plantation and listened carefully to stories he was told there. Becoming a reporter and journalist when he grew up, Harris quickly learned that the public liked to read these old stories told by the African American friends of his youth. Chandler wrote and published the tales in the vernacular or speech of the African American slaves from whom he first heard them. The tales have been rewritten many times by many writers to help readers better enjoy the story of competition of various sorts between familiar animals. In the tar baby story, a fox tries to outwit a rabbit, and the rabbit manages to get away in the end. The contrasts of the different versions is interesting. Harris attempted to record the vernacular of the slaves as he recalled it. His spelling is sometimes archaic, but there is a rich flavor in the choice of words and dialect. Another writer, Julius Lester, wrote a more accessible version for today's readers, and his version was richly illustrated by Jerry Pinkney.

The focus of the story was a tar baby that the fox set up beside the road. The rabbit tried to get the tar baby to respond to friendly greetings, the tar baby didn't, and the rabbit finally became so angry at the tar baby's silence that he swung at it with hands, feet, and his head, and finally got stuck. Harris wrote, "'Ef you don't lemme loose, I'll knock you again,' sez Brer Rabbit, sezee, en wid dat he fotch 'er a wipe wid de udder han', en dat stuck. Tar-Baby, she ain't sayin' nothin', en Brer Fox, he lay low" (Chase 1983: 7). Julius Lester told that part of the tale like this: "'You let me go!' Brer Rabbit yelled. 'Let me go or I'll really pop you one.' He twisted and turned, but he couldn't get loose. 'All right! I warned you!' And he smacked the Tar Baby on the other side of its head. BIP! His other fist was stuck" (Lester 1987: 14).

The story ends with the rabbit caught by the fox, but then escaping anyway. The fox threatens to barbecue, hang, or skin the wily rabbit, and the rabbit agrees that all those deaths would be better than another fate he could think of. The worst thing that could happen, the rabbit teases and says to the fox, would be that the fox would toss him into the briar patch. Repeating this "fear" over and over, the fox decides that he really wants to do the worst thing to the rabbit that he might do, and so, as Lester wrote, "He snatched him off the Tar Baby and wound up his arm like he was trying to throw a fast ball past

"Ef you don't lemme loose I'll knock you agin!"

Brer Rabbit determined to get the Tar Baby to talk.

Hank Aaron and chunked that rabbit across the road and smack dab in the middle of the briar patch" (16).

In the Harris version, the rabbit says, "'Skin me, BrerFox,' sez Brer Rabbit, sezee, 'snatch out my eyeballs, t'ar out my years by de roots, en cut off my legs,' sezee, 'but do please, Brer Fox, don't fling me in dat brier patch,' sezee" (Polley 1978: 262). And again, Brer Fox "cotch 'im by de behime legs en slung 'im right in de middle er de brier patch" (262). In the end, the rabbit is safely far from the fox. He turns and waves to the fox and says, "'I was born and raised in the briar patch, Brer Fox! Born and raised in the briar patch!' And he hopped over the hill and out of sight" (Lester 1987: 16).

VARIATIONS OF PROSE NARRATIVES

Complex Tales

In an earlier world, many long, complicated stories were memorized by tellers and passed along from generation to generation to preserve cultural traditions and beliefs. Two of theses ancient stories, one called *Gilgamesh,* a story about a king who ruled in southern Iraq (ancient Sumeria) in a walled city called Urak, and the other called *Ramayana,* from India, a story of an exiled heir-to-the-throne, have been carefully preserved in a variety of ways. The story of Gilgamesh, thought to be one of the oldest extended narratives of human history, was told as an oral poem as early as 2200 B.C.E. The oldest copy of the complex Gilgamesh poem was written on clay tablets in cuneiform lettering, and it is thought to be from 2000 B.C.E.

The following is a summary of the Gilgamesh story written by Margaret Fleming. This summary includes the important elements of the narrative, but good translations of the longer versions are richer and more complex.

Gilgamesh is god and man; Enkidu is animal and man. In this epic, they become human together. Gilgamesh, King of Uruk, sleeps with all the virgins but has no real friend. Enkidu lives with animals until Gilgamesh sends a prostitute to teach him human ways. When Enkidu comes to Uruk, Gilgamesh is afraid of him. They fight, but suddenly each sees himself in the other's eyes, and they become friends.

Together they go the Forest of Cedar to find and kill the Evil One. Enkidu knows the forest is dangerous and is afraid, but Gilgamesh encourages him. They kill the Evil One, but Enkidu is wounded. Upon their return, the goddess Ishtar offers herself as a bride to Gilgamesh, who refuses her. Angered, she has her father send the Bull of Heaven to kill him, but Enkidu kills the Bull, even though his former wound has not healed. This effort further weakens him, and he soon dies.

Gilgamesh is inconsolable. Trying to regain his friend or to understand his loss, he journeys to seek the wise man Utnapishtim, who dwells beyond the Sea of Death. In his grief and rage Gilgamesh smashes the sacred stones that could have helped him. Finally, however, a boatman ferries him across, and he is able to talk with Utnapishtim, who tells him the following story.

The gods decided to create a great flood. They told Utnapishtim to build a ship and to take inside all his family and the seed of all the animals. He did so, and the floods came. After seven days the water subsided, and Utnapishtim saw dead bodies everywhere. He could not understand or accept this until the god Ea made him and his wife like gods and took them to live alone at the end of the earth.

Gilgamesh cannot receive any comfort from this story. Utnapishtim says he has no wisdom to give him, but he orders the boatman to burn the pelts that remind Gilgamesh of his friend and to return him to the other shore. As Gilgamesh leaves, Utnapishtim tells him of a plant growing in the river that will prick him with its thorns but will give him new life. Gilgamesh finds it, plucks it, and returns to the other shore, where he stops to refresh himself in a pool, leaving the plant unguarded. While he is bathing, a serpent comes and eats the plant. Gilgamesh returns to find only the serpent's discarded skin. He goes back to Uruk, but finds no one to share his sorrow [He reigns as king and writes the story of his quest.]. (Fleming 1974: 15–16)

The *Ramayana* was written down from oral lore by the Indian sage Valmiki in Sanskrit some time between the second century B.C.E. and the second century C.E., and parts of it are still memorized in the course of traditional Indian education. The plot of the *Ramayana,* taken from Valmiki's text and condensed by Wendy Doniger, can be summarized as follows:

> Sita, the wife of Prince Rama, had been born from a
> furrow of the earth. The demon king Ravana stole Sita
> from Rama and kept her captive on the island of Lanka
> for many years. Rama enlisted the help of an army of
> monkeys and finally killed Ravana and brought Sita back
> home with him. But then he said he feared that his
> people worried that Sita's reputation if not her chas-
> tity, has been sullied by her long sojourn in the house
> of another man. He forced Sita to undergo an ordeal
> by fire: she swore that she had always been faithful to
> Rama, called on the fire to protect her, and entered the
> blazing flame; but the god of Fire placed her in Rama's
> lap, assuring him that Sita had always been pure in
> thought as well as deed. Rama reinstated her, but when
> he doubted her again she disappeared forever back into
> the earth. (Doniger 2002: 105)

Märchen and Conte Fabulaire

These short stories or fabulous tales are told the world over. One typical example of a Märchen or *conte fabulaire* is the popular tale of "Snow White."

The animated film version of "Snow White" was made by the Walt Disney Studio, and it was their first feature-length animated film. This story was one of the tales collected in Germany and published in German by the Brothers Grimm. The following is a brief summary.

> This tale is about a jealous stepmother who plotted to kill Snow White, a gorgeous young girl. It is also about the seven dwarfs who loved, protected, and cared for the girl. The evil queen vainly tried to be the prettiest ("fairest") in the land. To determine the reigning beauty, she consulted her omniscient talking mirror. She tried many different ways to kill Snow White, but was unsuccessful. A prince from a neighboring kingdom saved Snow White and married her. (Adler 1995: 126)

James Finn Garner has taken liberties with traditional Märchen and *conte fabulaire* tales. His *Politically Correct Bedtime Stories* have spoofed many of the tales, and "Snow White" is no exception. For instance, in the original English translation, the disturbing message from the talking mirror to the queen is: "Thou art fairer than all who are here, Lady Queen, But more beautiful still is Snow-white, as I ween" (Stern 1972: 250). Garner wrote: "Alas, if worth be based on beauty, Snow White has surpassed you, cutie" (Garner1994: 45). In another place, Garner wrote that the mirror replied: "Your weight is perfect for your shape and height, But for sheer OOOOMPH!, You can't beat Snow White" (51). In the resolution of Garner's version, Snow White and the queen open a "womyn's" spa and hire the prince as "a cute but harmless tennis pro" (56).

Fables

A fable is a simple ethical or moral folktale that often features animals as the primary characters. Aesop, a slave in ancient Greece and credited with gathering and telling many fables, told the story of "The Fox and the Crow," and that story has been retold by many tellers (and writers) over time. The character of the fox became well known for its ingenious and trickster characteristics, and in Europe,

> The fox, with his name today spelled Reynard, was the wily, unscrupulous, lying, immoral, and traitorous central figure in a series of fables satirizing life and politics in medieval Europe. He was beloved by the people of Germany, France, the Netherlands, and then England because he defied tricked, and made a mockery of the ideals and institutions of the day. (Dolan 1992: 165)

The fables told about the fox were metaphorical allegories for the times. The following version of "The Fox and the Crow" comes from a collection of Aesop's fables that originally published in 1894.

The fox tricked the crow out of the morsel of cheese.

The Fox and the Crow

A Fox once saw a Crow fly off with a piece of cheese in its beak and settle on a branch of a tree. "That's for me, as I am a Fox," said Master Renard, and he walked up to the foot of the tree. "Good-day, Mistress Crow," he cried. "How well you are looking to-day: how glossy your feathers; how bright your eye. I feel sure your voice must surpass that of other birds, just as your figure does; let me hear but one song from you that I may greet you as the Queen of Birds." The Crow lifted up her head and began to caw her best, but the moment she opened her mouth the piece of cheese fell to the ground, only to be snapped up by Master Fox. "That will do," said he. "That was all I wanted. In exchange for your cheese I will give you a piece of advice for the future—Do not trust flatterers. The Flatterer doth rob by stealth his victim, both of Wit and Wealth. (Jacobs 1966: 20–21)

Lori Langer de Ramírez wrote a short version of La Fontaine's "The Crow and the Fox" fable and posted it on the Internet.

> The fox wanted some
> Cheese that the crow had
> In his mouth, so he
> Complimented the crow.
> When the crow opened
> His mouth to respond, he
> Let the cheese fall. When
> The cheese hit the
> Ground, the fox ate it and
> Was very happy.
> (Ramírez 2005: 1)

Animal Tales

There are many folktales in the Chinese culture, and animals are often used as metaphors for phenomena of nature. Howard Giskin and his wife, Vicki, taught in China and collected many tales from their students. Giskin stated that, "The Chinese are very fond of such tales, telling them to their children, their grandchildren, and even their friends" (Giskin 1997: ix). These tellers are not professional storytellers or folklorists, but rather, they are people who have heard the tales since their childhood and pass them along casually as they are remembered. Their performances are informal and unrehearsed. This animal tale about a big wave was told to the Giskins by their student Chen Lihua, who was raised in a small town near the coastal city of Hangzhou, in the Zhejiang Province.

> Long, long ago, there was a dragon king who lived under the Qiantang River. He was the ruler of all the creatures living in the sea, and he had a son who was a green dragon, as well as a very old tortoise as a helper.
>
> These dragons had magical powers, of course, so every year on August 15 of the lunar calendar, the old dragon and his son would make the river angry. The water would surge over the bank, destroying houses and flooding the fields. At the same time, the dragons would ride a beautiful wagon on the surge, watching the people suffer from the flood. As the dragons did this they were very happy because of the people's misery. The people hated them, but nothing could be done.
>
> At that time there happened to be a white tiger sleeping near the river. This was not a normal tiger, but a magical one who had slept for hundreds of years. When the cries of the people finally awakened him, he became very angry.

"How can that old fellow do that!" he shouted. Wanting to punish the dragon, he waited near the river until the day of the surge.

Finally the day came, but this time only the young dragon and the old tortoise rode the wave happily while the people were crying and moaning. With anger in his eyes, the white tiger arched his back and jumped into the river just in front of the dragon. The dragon's horses stopped suddenly, causing the dragon to nearly fall off his wagon.

"Who are you?" the dragon shouted. "How dare you do this to me?"

The tiger in turn shouted angrily, "You needn't ask that!"

"You—you get out of my way! Do you know who I am? I'm the son of the dragon king."

"Yes, I know," replied the tiger. "You are the one I've come to kill."

The tiger lunged at the dragon and a fight began. They fought day after day, neither able to gain the advantage over the other. Eventually the dragon began to tire. As the dragon weakened, the tortoise bit the tiger's tail, causing the tiger to lose strength. The dragon once again became strong while the tiger started to lose the battle.

At that critical moment, a demigod named Lu Dongbing happened to come across the dragon and the tiger fighting. Wondering what was happening, he asked a passerby to explain. Wanting to help the people get rid of the dragon, Lu Dongbing heaved his sword into the air, which struck the dragon on the head and killed him. The great creature fell to the ground and turned into a mountain—Green Dragon Mountain. Though safe now, the tiger was so badly wounded from the fight that he too died, changing into another mountain—White Tiger Mountain.

Seeing what had happened, the tortoise wanted to escape so he tried to walk away very quietly. Lu Dongbing flung his scabbard at the tortoise striking him on the back and killing him. The tortoise became a third mountain—Tortoise Mountain.

These three mountains sit near the bank of the Qiantang River. After the terrible fight between the white tiger and the green dragon, the surge became weaker and the river never again flooded the fields. (16–18)

Trickster Tales

The ancient trickster figure, Hermes, is one of the oldest in Western literature. Hermes, as is frequently the case with tricksters, could be beneficially deceitful. He aided the gods and consistently pulled a variety of tricks. According to Ovid, a Roman writer, Hermes could talk like a metronome and told stories to the thousand-eyed monster until he fell asleep.

On the day of his birth, Hermes invented the lyre after killing a tortoise he met. He made the instrument from the shell. That same first day of life, he stole 50 cows from Apollo and made them walk backwards so they would not leave a trail that could be followed. After he did all that, he returned to his cradle!

When Apollo was told who had stolen his cattle he was angry, but Hermes charmed him with the gift of the lyre, and Apollo ended up awarding him instead of creating a punishment. Hermes, a popular god of luck and wealth in the ancient world, was also the god of thieves and fertility. Zeus, the father of both Apollo and Hermes, was amused by his clever baby son and made

Hermes trying to pass by Cerberus, the multi-headed guard dog of Hades.

him guardian of the roads and patron of travelers. "He was a messenger or herald of the gods, and conductor of the souls of the dead to Hades. . . . He was also the god of sleep and dreams. He is represented with wings on his sandals, a broad-brimmed hat . . . and a staff on which serpents are twined. . . . Hermes was identified by the Romans with their god Mercury" (Harvey 1986: 205).

Folk Narrative

The Chinese tale about the tiger, the dragon, and the tortoise is a folk narrative. As it usually defined, a folk narrative is simply an oral, prose story that has been repeated a few times and consequently exists in more than one version. In our world of storytellers, collectors, and folklorists, many of the folk narratives have been recorded, but many have been lost. Some folk narratives are accompanied by pictures, and throughout the world, there are ancient traditions of illustrating stories in different ways. Picture storytelling was a style used in Java, and the Chinese writer, Ying-yai Sheng-lan wrote in 1416:

> There is a sort of men who paint on paper men, birds, animals, insects and so on; the paper is like a scroll and is fixed between two wooden rollers three feet high; at one side these rollers are level with the paper, whilst they protrude at the other side. The man squats down on the ground and places the picture before him, unrolling one part after the other and turning it towards the spectators, whilst in the native language and in a loud voice he gives an explanation of every part; the spectators sit around him and listen, laughing or crying according to what he tells them. (Coomaraswamy 1929: 186)

One of the methods of telling folk narratives in Japan is called *kamishibai*. A wooden frame is used to display a series of large, sturdy cards that have pictures on one side and the story written on the back. The frame is often set up on the teller's bicycle. For many years these street tellers were the only entertainment available to children. The cards are slowly slid to the side and placed in the back of the stack, and the story is read or told. One of the *kamishibai* stories tells about an old couple who barely have enough food or money to survive. This story has many folkloric elements and motifs. To begin with, it is performed orally. It describes material cultural artifacts of the stone statues, handwoven cloth and hats, it is about celebrating New Year's Eve, a customary holiday. It also represents a belief system in the folk belief in the deity Jizo.

Hats for the Jizos

On New Year's Eve, a poor, old man goes to the village hoping to sell some cloth that his wife has woven so he can buy some special food to celebrate the New Year. No one is interested in buying the cloth, however, and just to have something different to take home he exchanges the cloth for five hand made straw hats another man has been trying to sell.

On the way home, the old man sees six statues of the deity Jizo who appear to be cold and suffering because they are covered with snow. The old man decides to cover their bare heads using the five straw hats and his own scarf.

When he arrives home, he tells his wife what he saw and what he did. The old woman approves of what her husband had done. The couple celebrate the New Year with the simple food they usually eat and go to bed early. During the night, they are awakened by strange chanting sounds that seem to come from far away. The voices grow louder, and the old couple hears the voices say something about the hats for the Jizos. Suddenly there is a loud boom, as though something heavy was dropped. The old couple were very afraid. Then the voices faded away.

After everything had returned to a cold silence, the old woman and old man cracked open their front door to see if they could figure out what the noise was. On their step was a huge straw bag with wonderful gifts flowing from it. They pulled the gift into the warmth of their little home, and out spilled golden coins, rice cakes, fine fish, silken kimonos, and other fine foods and presents. This was their reward from the six Jizos, and the old man and old women lived happily ever after. (Matsutani 1995: 1–16)

Personal Narrative

Linda Dégh reminded us that "People tell personal narratives to be listened to" (Dégh 1995: 39). The following personal narrative is from an experience the author of this text had in northern Spain. After a long, winding hike in the Pyrenees Mountains, our group of 13 students became disoriented and quite lost. We climbed and wound around through some of the lower hills of the Pyrenees until we happened upon a meadow and could hear the sound of sheep. They were wearing copper bells and foraging in the brush out of our sight. Because we were quite lost, we decided to follow the sheep further up the hill to see if we could find the sheepherder and be given directions back to a road. We were hoping to find someone who could direct or even lead us out of the maze of trees and jutting rocks.

In an opening beside a deep forest, we emerged to find a herder's hutlike cottage. He was there with a few friends and saw us coming. We had our own supplies (bread, salami, fruit, and water), but he insisted that we share his food. He split a small quarter-round of golden-colored sheep cheese that he said he had made himself; I watched him deftly cut thin slices with a razor-sharp pocketknife and hand it to us, one-by-one. There was a coarse white bread, a few crackers, a little red and white wine, two Cokes, and two beers from his hut that he shared with our group. His hands were deep brown and his face was lined with dark mysteries, but his eyes twinkled with delight at this haggard group of mountain-climbing Americans. He spoke Basque and Spanish and offered us ancient hospitality. We received it with delight and relief, and he pointed us in the right direction when we left.

An experience like that echoes with deep memories of ancient host/guest cordialities, and in such a primeval, pastoral setting it was as though we had stepped into some sort of time warp. (Thursby 2004:190–91)

As we turned away from him, he raised his hand in a gesture of goodbye and in blessing for our unpredictable journey. Stopping to look for the folkloric items in this short personal narrative, it is again easy to find evidence of the four basic elements: oral, material, customary, and belief. The old sheepherder greeted us verbally in traditional Basque, "*Ongi, zer meduz?*" The typical greeting means, essentially, "Hello, how are you?" He offered us the golden sheep cheese, made by his own hands—a material item created from his knowledge of traditional food production. He had inherited and practiced the ancient custom of welcoming strangers to his "hearth," and he provided humble sustenance for our pleasure. He blessed us as we left, giving evidence of his traditional belief system.

Novella

A novella is a tale or short story especially used by early Italian and French writers. It was from this form that the novel as we know it today was developed. A famous example of the novella is Giovanni Boccaccio's *Decameron,* a frame tale with its setting in the plague-ridden city of Florence. Boccaccio (1313–75) did not respect this work because he wrote it for relaxation and escape at a dismal time of his life.

It is the story of ten young nobles (seven women and three men) who withdraw from the city of Naples to the healthier climate of the suburbs. Trying to kill time as they wait for the threat of the plague to pass, each of them agrees to tell a story on each of the ten days they are spending there.

Boccaccio made the tale more interesting by including folkloric elements of descriptions, behaviors, folk dancing and songs. Though the work has a bawdy reputation, a reader looking for scandalous stories will have to sort through, about three to one, between innocent stories and those which are really ribald. My favorite of the stories is one that tells about thwarted love. The fifth story told on the fourth day, abridged and paraphrased below, it is one of the innocent stories of love and tragic death.

> Once upon a time, long, long ago, a young man and young woman fell deeply in love. He was of the common class, and she, Lisabetta, was a member of an aristocratic family. Observing the romance, her brothers decided to rid the family of this unwelcome lover. They tricked him into going on a trip with him, killed him, and buried him in an hidden place in the woods.
>
> The young woman missed him, of course, and thought that in spite of all his promises, he had deserted her. Then she had a dream. She learned through the dream that he had been murdered and buried. The dream also revealed to her where he had been buried. She enlisted a discreet handmaiden to assist her and went and found the body. Taking the head back to her home, she placed it in a large, ornate flower pot, covered it with soil, and planted aromatic basil in the soil. Tending it carefully, she wept a long time each day and slowly lost her reason as the basil flourished in the rich soil.
>
> Eventually her brothers took the basil and pot away from her, and the final tragedy in this little tale was that the maiden soon died of grief. Sadly, there was no "Happily ever after"!

Frame Tale

The frame tale, as described above in the discussion of Boccaccio's *Decameron,* is a story within as story. One of the stories recounted in the ancient Arabian story tale of the *Thousand and One Nights,* told by the Princess Sheherazade to the King, is "The Story of 'Ali Baba and the Forty Thieves." A paraphrased version follows, but it shares only the highlights of this delightful, folklore-filled tale. This is only one of the many tales told in the *Thousand and One Nights,* also called a frame tale because it is a series of stories told by the Princess Sheherazade to entertain the king night after night.

Long ago, two brothers named Kasim and 'Ali Baba lived in a town in Persia. Their father gave them each equal amounts of a small inheritance, but the brothers lived quite differently. Kasim married a rich wife and 'Ali Baba married a poor one. Each day 'Ali Baba took his three donkeys into the forest, cut wood, and sold the wood in town to earn enough money to survive.

One day 'Ali Baba observed a band of thieves, 40 in number, ride into the forest and hide their loot in a cave. 'Ali Baba heard them command a rock covering the opening of the cave to move by saying the words "Open Simsin" (or "Open Sesame," a more common command used in contemporary versions of the story). The band of thieves entered the cave, and the rock closed behind them. After a long while they emerged, and the leader turned toward the rock and shouted, "Shut, Sesame!"

After they had been gone a long time, 'Ali Baba decided to try to see if the commands would work for him. The first command did work, and inside the cave 'Ali Baba found all sorts of splendid provisions: silks, gold and silver, and

The forty thieves Ali Baba observed at the door of the cave of treasures. *North Wind Picture Archives.*

bags of money. He loaded his three donkeys with as much bounty as he could, covered it with wood, and left the cave. Both commands worked easily for him.

He secretly shared his good fortune with his wife. Wanting to know how much gold there was, the wife borrowed a measure from her brother-in-law Kasim. The wealthy wife, eager to know what 'Ali Baba's wife was measuring, put some suet in the bottom of the measure so some of the weighed material would stick to it. When the measure was returned, the rich wife learned that it was gold and immediately informed her husband.

Kasim questioned 'Ali Baba about the source of the wealth, and was told the truth. The next day, Kasim arose early and went to the forest cave that his brother had described. He took many mules in order to retrieve as much of the treasure as he could. He found the cave, gave the command, and entered. He was so excited about the treasure, however, that he forgot the command to make the rock open again. Unable to leave the cave, he paced back and forth within it trying to remember the command.

Meanwhile, the band of thieves returned and Kasim heard them arrive. Rushing out as soon as the rock moved and the opening was uncovered, Kasim attacked the leader but the other robbers killed him. In order to frighten other possible thieves of the thieves, they cut Kasim's body into four parts and hung them just inside the cave. Then they left to continue their work of attacking caravans for plunder. When Kasim did not arrive home that night, his wife became worried and went to 'Ali Baba for help. Upon hearing her anxiety, he went to the cave and found his brother. He covered his brother with cloth and loaded him on one of his donkeys. He piled bags of gold on the other two (again covering them carefully with wood for secrecy) and returned to the town.

Realizing that deceit would be the best way to handle the new widow, 'Ali Baba and one of his brother's housemaids devised a way to make it appear that Kasim was very, very ill. They found a shoemaker to sew the body back together, and Kasim was buried according to the custom of the day. The wife did not suspect foul play; however, when the thieves returned to the cave and found that the interloper's body had been removed, they knew there must be an accomplice and set out to determine who it was. One of the robbers volunteered to be the investigator.

Eavesdropping in the town led them to the shoemaker. The shoemaker, in turn, led them to the door of Kasim's home (where 'Ali Baba now lived). The robber marked the house with a piece of chalk, and then they both went their ways. The housemaid had been out when this occurred, but when she returned she noticed the mark. Thinking that it was an ill omen, she marked several houses on either side in the same way and said nothing about it.

When the troop of robbers made their way secretly to the house, they found several marked houses, and the plan was foiled. Putting the first volunteer investigator to death, they sent another who, pursuing the same trail successfully, marked Kasim's house with red chalk in an obscure place. The housemaid, who missed nothing, again saw the mark and subsequently marked several houses on either side in the same manner in an obscure place with red chalk. Failing again, the second investigator was put to death. The captain and troop of robbers were frustrated and angry by this time. The captain went to the town this time, followed the same trail of information, and memorized the look of the house instead of marking it. Then he obtained 19 mules loaded with 38 jars. The robbers climbed into 37 of the jars, and the thirty-eighth was filled with oil.

Boldly, the captain road into town with this entourage and went directly to 'Ali Baba's home seeking refuge for the night. Abiding the ancient customs of hospitality and not recognizing the captain of the thieves, 'Ali Baba opened the gates to his courtyard and welcomed in the captain and what appeared to be mules loaded with 38 jars of oil. The housemaid assisted her guest, the captain, to his room and then realized that the house was completely out of oil and there was no light. She went to the courtyard to fill a large vessel with oil but when she opened the first jar, the robber within asked if it was time to attack. She immediately realized the situation. She told him that it was not, and then she went to each jar and whispered the same message. Then she devised a plan unknown to 'Ali Baba, her master.

The housemaid returned to the house and prepared a large pot of boiling oil. Returning to the courtyard, she poured enough into each lidded jar to smother and kill each of the hidden robbers, then she returned to the house and quietly sat by the window to see what would happen next. She heard the captain tossing pebbles at the jars just before dawn to awaken the men for the attack. Not receiving any response, he checked the jars, found his men all dead, and fearing that his plan had been discovered, fled over the wall of the garden. When 'Ali Baba arose, the housemaid took him to the garden and explained the whole story. They buried the bodies and weapons of the men in the soft soil in the back of the garden, and the men's mules were sold in the market over time.

The captain determined that he would not be undone. He designed a ruse in order to deceive and murder 'Ali Baba. Pretending to be a merchant, he set up a warehouse just opposite to Kasim's house where 'Ali Baba's son had his business. Soon he became a friendly and trusted associate of 'Ali Baba's son and was taken to 'Ali Baba's home, and making a good impression, was invited to stay for dinner. He said he could not because he could not eat food prepared with salt. 'Ali

Baba told the housemaid to prepare food without salt for their guest, and the housemaid became curious and suspicious. She peeked to see who the guest was and recognized the captain; further, she saw that he was armed.

The housemaid, a beautiful woman, arrayed herself as an exotic dancer and performed an elaborate dance for the diners. At an unguarded moment, she plunged a dagger into the heart of the captain. She quickly explained to 'Ali Baba and his son who the guest was, and further that because he would not eat salt with 'Ali Baba, salt being a symbol of trust between people, she suspected foul intentions from the moment she received the dinner order. 'Ali Baba was so astounded with all that this bright and beautiful housemaid had done for him and his family, that he suggested that she become the wife of his son. That suggestion was accepted with joy, and they all lived moderately but with good fortune in great honor and splendor until the time of their deaths (Eliot, Lane, and Lane-Poole 2001: n.p.).

An interesting note on this passage is the word *Simsim* in the original translation rather than the more familiar *Sesame*.

> This talismanic word, though it is the Arabic name of sesamé (*Sesamum orientale,* a plant producing oil-grain much used in the East), must have some other meaning. A German folk-tale, "Simeliberg," beginning in something of the same way with the magical opening of a rock, has the phrase "Open simsi," which the Grimms explain as an old German word for "mountain" (Hartland, Inst. Folklore Congress, 1891). There is nothing to prove that 'Ali Baba is not a European folk-tale turned into Arabic. . . .(2001: n.p.)

Formula Tale

A formula tale, familiar to folklorists and storytellers in the United States, usually involves repetition. The most common, as mentioned above, is "The House That Jack Built." George Schoemaker gave the example: "This is the house that Jack built. This is the malt that lay in the house that Jack built" (1990: 234). Other formula tales are called endless tales because they circle around and around to the beginning. Shoemaker gave this example for the endless tale:

> Once upon a time as we sat around the campfire telling funny tales, a stranger rode into our mi[d]st on an old grey mule, and we said, "Stranger, tell us a funny tale," and he began something like this: 'Once upon a time as we sat around the campfire telling funny tales, a stranger rode into our mi[d]st on an old grey mule, and we said, "Stranger, tell us a funny tale," and he began something like this . . . " (235)

Ballad

A ballad is usually a story that is sung. One of the most well known tunes in the United States is that of the ballad "Greensleeves." William Chatterton Dix wrote a Christmas carol, *What Child Is This* and set it to the traditional English melody. The tune actually appeared first in 1652, and, although it has not been verified, legend has it that Henry VIII wrote it for Anne Boleyn during their courtship around 1530. "There is an entry in the Stationers' Register in 1580 licensing Richard Jones to print *A new Northern Dittye of the Lady Green-Sleeves*" (Taylor: n.p.). The lyrics of *What Child Is This* are found in most Christmas songbooks in the United States.

Proverb

Folklorist Jan Brunvand wrote that a "true proverb is always a complete sentence, varies slightly in form, and usually expresses some general truth or wisdom. Such sayings are termed 'fixed phrase' kinds of oral folklore, and the variation comes in their meanings and uses in particular contexts" (Brunvand 1998: 93). Proverbs often express a general truth found in every culture around the world. Following are some less-known Basque proverbs collected by Rita Wasil for her master's thesis:

Its own nest is lovely to every bird.

There is no small quantity that will not reach all; nor is there any large quantity that will not terminate.

As turbulent and muddy as his water is, never say, of it I shall not drink.

While herding sheep, I give orders to my dog . . . and he to his tail. (1970: 486–87)

Memorate

A memorate is usually defined as a first-person account of an individual's personal encounter with the supernatural, though many of these stories are passed along and become part of folklore. Linda Dégh wrote that, "People believe their own senses first. 'It happened to me,' began 79-year-old Nick Mészáros in his account of how he accidentally entered the magic circle at midnight on his way home and learned the secret of eternal youth" (Dégh 2001: 67).

Memorate stories are told throughout the world, and in the Asian tradition, many beliefs in the supernatural surface in the telling of these stories. In Siberia, in the far north of eastern Europe, there are many tales about the *leshii,* which are supernatural spirits of the woods who can lead travelers astray. This old tale from eastern Europe has a happy but unexplained ending.

The Happy Hostage

One day, a young girl wandered off into the forest and disappeared. Despite their best efforts, family and friends failed to find her and eventually gave her up for dead. Three years went by before a hunter from the girl's village happened to find himself in the same sector of the woods. There, on a log across the path, he saw an odd-looking spirit. Realizing that this was a *leshii,* the hunter quickly raised his gun and fired. He saw the *leshii* fall then crawl off into the undergrowth. So the hunter followed.

The trail led to a hut in a clearing and inside the hut he saw the *leshii,* stretched out in death, and beside him a young woman weeping. When the hunter asked her who she was, she looked at him blankly: so he took her to his village where her parents recognized the daughter they had lost long ago. At first she could not understand anything he told her, all memory of her life among humans wiped away. Slowly, however, she recovered. She married the hunter and they lived happily together for many years. As they got older, they would wander in the forest, looking for the hut where she had been confined. Yet though they searched high and low they could not find it: it had vanished as if it had never existed. (Kerrigan 1999: 73)

Humorous Anecdote

Américo Paredes, a folklorist, wrote an article called "Folk Medicine and the Intercultural Jest." In the article, Paredes talks about the skilled *curanderos,* or folk doctors, among the Mexican people. A humorous anecdote that Paredes shared from his anonymous Informant No. 24, Brownsville, Texas, October 20, 1962, though a little scatological, follows:

They tell about an old man who was a *curandero,* that they brought him a patient who was sick in the stomach. And he said, "Give him goat turds."

[He] Said, "But what do you mean, give him goat turds!"

"Yes," he said, "Boiled."

Well, so they did it, and the man got well. And then there was a meeting of physicians. Said, [he] "Listen, man," he said. "We never could find out what was wrong with him. And he got well with goat turds."

So they called the old *curandero.* Said [he], "Well, why did you give goat turds to this man?

He said, "It's very simple. Because I knew the ailment he had," he said, "could be cured with some sort of herb. But I didn't know which one," he said.

"And since goats eat all kinds of weeds and herbs, I knew the plant needed would be there in the s—t." (Paredes 1990: 68)

Tall Tale

These short, humorous narratives are based on exaggeration. They are also known as "windies," "whoppers," and just plain lies. They come from all over the world and are often related to male-dominated pastimes and occupations. Gerald Thomas, a Newfoundland folklorist, shared some Newfoundland fishermen tall tales:

> Fishermen in Newfoundland tell of the reef they hauled their dory onto in order to light a fire and boil their kettle, only to discover, as they are leaving, that the reef was, in fact, a whale. Others tell of a pond or river in which they were wading while playing a particularly large fish and how, on grabbing some tufts of grass to pull themselves out, they discover they have, in face, caught a brace of hares; in addition, their hipwaders have filled with eels while they were struggling with their initial catch. (1996: 700)

Joke

The punch line is the clincher for a good, narrative joke. If the punch line is flubbed, then the humor is lost. Some tellers are very good at weaving jokes into their stories, and often jokes arise in light conversation by using double meanings or unexpected comments. Knock-knock jokes are particularly exchanged in children's culture, and Simon Bronner suggested that they are used sometimes to remind children to press strangers for their identity. A few listed in his *American Children's Folklore* are:

> Knock, knock.—who's there? Doughnut.—Doughnut who?—Doughnut talk to strangers knocking at your door. Knock, knock.—Who's there?—Sarah.— Sarah who?—Sarah doctor in the house? Knock, knock.—Who's there?— Banana.—Banana who?—Knock, knock.—Who's there?—Banana.—Banana who?—Knock, knock.—Who's there?—Banana.—Banana who?—Knock, knock.—Who's there?—Orange.—Orange who?—Orange ya glad I didn't say banana? (1988: 118–19)

Catch Joke

In Jan Brunvand's *Study of American Folklore,* the following example of a catch riddle is given:

What's the first sign of insanity?

    —Hair growing on your knuckles.

    Then as the dupe sneaks a look at the back of his hand, the riddler [subject] asks, What's the second sign?

    —Looking for it. (1998: 123)

Riddle

William Pepicello and Thomas A. Green wrote that "riddles, as generally defined, must be answerable, though with difficulty, and must contain within themselves a basis for arriving at the answer, however disguised" (1984: 88). The conundrums and enigmatic questions posed to Alice by the Mad Hatter are impossible to answer because of the lack of clues. The question he posed, "Why is a raven like a writing desk?" is never answered, and Alice is left wondering and complaining about the unanswerable questions posed by adults.

Riddles appear throughout world literature. They are used in the Hebrew scriptures; for instance, Samson's riddling challenge to the Philistines in Judges 14:14. It states, "Out of the eater came forth meat, and out of the strong came forth sweetness"—Answer: A lion with honey in its carcass (Judg. 14:14). In Classical Sanskrit, the writing of the Indo-Indians, there are riddles and word puzzles of almost every kind imaginable. "A typical example is found in the *Subhāsitaratnabhāgāra:* "He has no feet, yet he travels far; literate, but no scholar he; no mouth, yet he clearly speaks. If you know him, you are wise. Answer: *lekhapatram,* a letter" (Salomon 1996: 169). In the tradition of ancient China, there were divination sources called *chia-ku-wen,* or oracle bone texts, found on tortoise shells or cow skulls. Unlike riddles from other ancient cultures, these were straight yes/no answers, but they involved guessing games that operated somewhat like riddles. When heated, these objects produced readable cracks and were interpreted by those allowed to do so as prophetic judgments (Keightley 1985: n.p.).

In the ancient world, both Western and Eastern, writers and dramatist have used riddles to capture the interest of the readers and to add tension and intrigue to their plots. One of the most famous riddles of all time is the one that the sphinx of Thebes posed: What walks on all fours in the morning, on two in the afternoon, and three in the evening? Oedipus, the sadly fated hero, knew the answer and became a ill-destined king: man crawls in the beginning, walks upright in his active life, and then uses a cane in his later years. Based on events and artifacts of everyday life, riddles provide another captivating oral folk venue for stimulating verbal interaction and interesting exchanges among humans.

Rhyme (Nursery Rhyme)

Because many of nursery rhymes are familiar, various literary writers, from before Shakespeare to the twentieth-century English mystery writer Agatha Christie and beyond have incorporated their motifs and themes in various dramas and books. "Ring around the Rosie," "Old King Cole," and "Deedle Deedle Dumpling" are typical nursery rhymes. *One Flew over the Cuckoo's Nest,* a novel by Ken Kesey that was made into a movie, adapted part of a counting rhyme for its title and theme. Storytellers often incorporate all or part of a nursery rhyme and other rhyme schemes and allusions in their presentations.

Limerick

Edward Lear (1812–88) was widely recognized for his limerick form of poetry as well as nonsense rhymes. He wrote the *Book of Nonsense and Nonsense Songs* (1846, 1855, 1861). It was the custom of the time not to place the author's name in children's books, so Edward Lear's name did not appear until the third edition in 1861, which was published in London by Routledge, Warne, and Routledge. The following is a limerick that appeared in the title page of the first edition:

> There was an Old Derry down Derry,
> [W]ho loved to see little folks merry;
> So he made them a book,
> [A]nd with laughter they shook
> [A]t the fun of that Derry down Derry.
> ("Edward Lear Home Page": n.p.)

Another of Lear's limericks, again with a place name in the first line:

> There was a young lady from Niger
> Who smiled as she rode on a tiger;
> They came back from the ride
> With the lady inside.
> And a smile on the face of the tiger.
> (Webster 1950: 253)

Puns

Though there are many examples, the following is a play on words from the play *Othello:*

Scene IV: enter DESDEMONA, EMILIA, and CLOWN

Des. Do you know, sirrah, where Lieutenant Cassio lies?

Clo. I dare not say he lies any where.

Des. Why, man?

Clo. He's a soldier, and for me to say a soldier lies, 'tis stabbing.

Des. Go to! where lodges he?

Clo. To tell you where he lodges, is to tell you where I lie.

Des. Can anything be made of this?

Clo. I know not where he lodges, and for me to devise a lodging and say he lies here, or he lies there, were to lie in mine own throat.

(Shakespeare 1974: 1225)

Most puns are unwritten. They are passing word games that are enjoyable to some who notice and play with them, and irritating to others who do not want to be distracted. The punning is voiced in such as ways as to play on two or more applications of the words, such as:

She sewed a seam
and sowed a dream.
Seamless her dream
(or so it did seem).
(Anonymous)

Shaggy Dog Story

Jan Brunvand gave an excellent example of a shaggy dog story ending in a pun:

Shaggy-dog stories continue to be invented, often to incorporate new characters or to allude to newly popular phrases. For instance, a shaggy-*frog* story was popular in the 1980s with Kermit the Frog (of the Muppets) entering the bank and asking Miss Paddywhack for a loan. As collateral he

Kermit has become an American media folk figure. *AP Wide World Photos.*

offers an odd triangular-shaped piece of polished wood with some wires connected to it. Miss Paddywhack takes the object in to the loan officer, who glances at it, and them stamps Kermit's application "Approved." When the teller in amazement asks what the object is, her boss replies, "It's a knicknack Paddywhack, give the frog a loan." (This time the phrase is an *old* one—a line from the English children's song "This Old Man" . . . (1998: 246)

Another, more literal shaggy dog story example was gathered from a personal interview with Denny Thursby, who had picked up the story years ago while living in the eastern part of the United States:

Once upon a time a wife expressed to her husband that she would really enjoy having a shaggy dog. The man went to the pet store and bought the shaggiest puppy they had. He took it home to her, and she said it really wasn't shaggy enough. He returned the dog and set out on a quest to find the shaggiest dog in town in order to please his wife.

The man tried other pet stores in the area, but every dog he took home to her failed to meet her expectations and had to be returned.

Finally, he learned that the shaggiest dogs in the United States were to be found in New York City. He hopped a plane and flew to New York, bought an extraordinarily shaggy puppy, and returned home with it.

He tied a ribbon around the neck of the puppy, fluffed it up as much as possible, and presented it to his wife.

"Oh no, honey," she exclaimed laughing, "that's much too shaggy"

Schwank

A schwank is a long story in which description of the characters or situation makes the narrative work rather than a closure or punch line. "Hawley's Yarn," given below, represents a schwank:

. . . Emboldened by his success, Hawley proceeded to relate that there was, in that same section, an area of twenty miles where the air was so pure that people never died, unless by accident.

"Never died!" exclaimed several of his hearers in astonishment.

"No gentlemen, it was quite possible. The rare purity of the atmosphere prevented it. When persons got too old to be useful, they would sometimes be blown away, and, once outside of the charmed circle, they were lost."

"Is that really possible?" asked one of his hearers, in some doubt.

"A fact upon my honor," rejoined old Hawley. "Indeed, some years ago several philanthropic gentlemen erected a museum at that place, where persons who became too old for usefulness were put into sacks, labeled, registered at the office, and hung up. If at any subsequent period their friends wished to converse with them, for a fee of fifty cents the old friend would be taken down, placed in a kettle of tepid water, and would soon be enabled to hold a conversation of a half an hour when he would be taken out, wiped off, and hung up again."

"That seems incredible!" remarked on of the listeners.

"Of course it does," replied Hawley. "It is nevertheless true. Why gentlemen," he continued, "on one occasion I went to the museum and asked if they had a subject there named Samuel Hawley. I had an uncle by that name who went to the Rocky Mountains thirty years before, and we had not heard from him in a long time. The clerk, having examined the register, replied that

Samuel Hawley was in Sack No. 367, and had been there nineteen years. I paid the fee and called for an interview. The contents of that particular sack were placed in the warm water, and in a short time I proceeded to tell my uncle who I was. He seemed pleased to see me, although I was a child when he left our part of the country. He inquired about my father and other friends. His voice was very weak, and after a conversation of about twenty minutes, he said his breath was failing him, and if I had nothing more to say he would like to be hung up again. I remarked that I believed he formerly owned a large gun, and asked him where it was. He informed me that it was lying on the cross-beam in my father's garret, and that I was welcome to it. I thanked him, and bidding him good-bye, the keeper of the museum took him in hand and soon placed him in his proper locality. If any of you should ever go that way, gentlemen, I hope you will call on my uncle and present him my compliments. Remember his number is 367." (Botkin 1989: 306, 307)

These examples of folkloric prose narrative are used in many ways in expressive culture. Folklorists have collected them from stories that wind back into antiquity. Some of the oral traditions have been written and archived, and many still remain alive and dynamic in our vernacular cultures around the world. There are many scholarly approaches to the study of prose narratives and the presence of folklore in the stories. While some folklorists focus on one area of oral folklore such as mythology, legend, or folktale, others may concentrate on studies of political philosophies and economic formations shaped by lore, and still others may spend a lifetime studying folk music, ballads, and/or folk dances. There are folklorists most interested in the oral lore and practices of specific holidays, while other folklorists are more interested in the artifacts and material representations of cultures that evidence traditionally transmitted arts and crafts. The next chapter will focus on some of the scholarship and approaches folklorists pursue in their study of the presence of folklore in story.

WORKS CITED

Adler, Bill, Jr. 1995. *Tell Me a Fairy Tale: A Parent's Guide to Telling Magical and Mythical Stories.* New York: Penguin.

Anonymous. "DigiTales—The Art of Telling Digital Stories." Available at: http://www.digitales.us/. Accessed 3 October 2005.

Barron, T. A. 2001. *A T. A. Barron Collection,* ed. Patricia Lee Gauch. New York: Philomel Books.

Boccaccio, Giovanni. 1995. *The Decameron.* Translated and with Introduction and Notes by C. H. McWilliam. 2d ed. New York: Penguin Books.

Botkin, B. A. [1944] 1989. *The Treasury of American Folklore: Stories, Ballads, and Traditions of the People.* New York: American Legacy Press.

Bronner, Simon J. 1988. *American Children's Folklore.* Little Rock, AR: August House.

Brunvand, Jan Harold. 1998. *The Study of American Folklore: An Introduction.* 4th ed. New York: W. W. Norton.

———. 2004. *Be Afraid, Be Very Afraid: The Book of Scary Urban Legends.* New York: W. W. Norton.

Chase, Richard. 1983. *The Complete Tales of Uncle Remus: Joel Chandler Harris.* Boston: Houghton Mifflin.

Coomaraswamy, Ananda. June 1929. "Picture Showmen." *Indian Historical Quarterly* 5 (2): 186.

Dégh, Linda. 1995. *Narratives in Society: A Performer-Centered Study of Narration.* Helsinki: Academia Scientiarum Fennica.

———. 2001. *Legend and Belief: Dialectics of a Folklore Genre.* Bloomington: Indiana University Press.

Dolan, Edward F. 1992. *Animal Folklore: From Black Cats to White Horses.* New York: Ivy Books.

Doniger, Wendy. 2002. "Ramayana." In *The Epic Voice,* ed. Alan D. Hodder and Robert E. Meagher, 102–27. Hampshire Studies in the Humanities. Westport, CT: Praeger Publishers.

"Edward Lear Home Page: A Book of Nonsense." Available at: http://www.nonsenselit.org/Lear/BoN/index.htmlAccessed 5 August 2005.

Ellis, Richard. *The Search for the Giant Squid.* New York: Penguin (Non-Classics), 1999.

Eliot, Charles William, Edward William Lane, and Stanley Lane-Poole. [1909–14] 2001. *Stories from the Thousand and One Nights.* The Harvard Classics, vol. 16. New York: P. F. Collier and Son. Available at http://www.bartleby.com/16/905.html, posted 2001. Accessed 14 September 2005.

Fleming, Margaret, ed. 1974. *Teaching the Epic.* Urbana, Illinois: National Council of Teachers of English.

Garner, James Finn. 1994. *Politically Correct Bedtime Stories: Modern Tales For Our Life and Times.* New York: Macmillan.

Giskin, Howard. 1997. *Chinese Folktales.* Lincolnwood, IL: NTC Publishing Group/Contemporary Publishing.

Harvey, Paul. 1986. *The Oxford Companion to Classical Literature.* New York: Oxford University Press.

Jacobs, Joseph, ed. [1894] 1996. *The Fables of Aesop.* New York: Schocken Books/Pantheon Books/Random House.

Keightley, David. 1985. *Sources of Shang History: The Oracle-Bone Inscriptions of Bronze-Age China.* Berkeley: University of California Press.

Kerrigan, Michael. 1999. "Spirit Masters and Little Demons." In *Myth and Mankind: Forests of the Vampire, Slavic Myth,* 58–79. London: Duncan Baird Publishers/Time-Life Books.

Laurel, Brenda. "A Tale about Some Crows." Digital Storytelling Association, Public News and Events. Available at http://www.dsaweb.org/04news_events/brenda.html. Accessed 3 October 2005.

Lee, Terry. 2003. "Journalist, Teacher, and Storyteller." *Points of Entry: Cross-Currents in Storytelling* 1 (1): 7–12.

Lester, Julius. 1987. *The Tales of Uncle Remus: The Adventures of Brer Rabbit.* New York: Dial Books.

Martin, Charles. 2005. *Ovid Metamorphoses.* Translation and Notes by Charles Martin. New York: W. W. Norton.

Matsutani, Miyoko. 1995. *Hats for the Jizos.* (Adaptation.) Kamishibai for Kids with permission from Doshinsha Co., Ltd. Japan.

Mayor, Adrienne. 2000. *The First Fossil Hunters: Paleontology in Greek and Roman Times.* Princeton, NJ: Princeton University Press.

Mintz, Jerome R. 1968. *Legends of the Hasidim: An Introduction to Hasidic Culture and Oral Tradition in the New World.* Chicago: University of Chicago Press.

Owen, James. 2005. "Holy Squid! Photos Offer First Glimpse of Live Deep-Sea Giant. *National Geographic News.* 9 September. Available at: http://news.nationalgeographic.com/news/2005/09/0927_050927_giant_squid.html. Accessed 3 October 2005.

Paredes, Américo. 1990. "Folk Medicine and the Intercultural Jest." In *Folk Groups and Folklore Genres: A Reader* ed. Elliott Oring, 63–77. Logan: Utah State University Press.

Pepicello, William, and Thomas A. Green. 1984. *The Language of Riddles.* Columbus: Ohio State University Press.

Polley, Jane, ed. 1978. *American Folklore and Legend.* Pleasantville, NY: The Reader's Digest Association.

Ramírez, Lori Langer de. 2005. Miscositas.com. Available at: *http://www.columbia.edu/~ljl17/fables3.html.* āccessed 6 October 2005.

Rule, Leslie. 2005. "Digital Storytelling." Available at http://electronicportfolios.com/digistory. Accessed 3 October 2005.

Salomon, Richard. 1996. "When Is a Riddle Not a Riddle? Some Comments on Riddling and Related Poetic Devices in Classical Sanskrit." In *Untying the Knot: On Riddles and Other Enigmatic Modes,* ed. Galit Hasan-Rokem and David Shulman, 168–78. New York: Oxford University Press.

Schenone, Laura. 2003. *A Thousand Years over a Hot Stove: A History of American Women Told through Food, Recipes, and Remembrances.* New York: W. W. Norton.

Schoemaker, George H. 1990. *The Emergence of Folklore in Everyday Life: A Fieldguide and Sourcebook.* Bloomington, Indiana: Trickster Press.

Shakespeare, William. 1974. *Othello.* In *The Riverside Shakespeare,* ed. G. Blakemore Evans, 1198–1248. Boston: Houghton Mifflin.

Smith, Paul. 1983. *The Book of Nasty Legends.* London: Routledge and Kegan Paul.

Stern, James, ed. 1972. *The Complete Grimm's Fairy Tales.* New York: Pantheon Books.

Taylor, Barry. "Greensleeves." Midi File 1. Available at: http://www.contemplator. com/england/grenslevs.html. Accessed 7 October 2005.

Thomas, Gerald. 1996. "Tall Tale." In *American Folklore: An Encyclopedia,* ed. Jan Harold Brunvand, 700–702. New York: Garland.

Thursby, Jacqueline S. 2004. "Culinary Tourism among Basques and Basque Americans: Maintenance and Inventions." In *Culinary Tourism* ed. Lucy Long, 186–205. Lexington: University Press of Kentucky.

Thury, Eva M., and Margaret K. Devinney. 2005. *Introduction to Mythology: Contemporary Approaches to Classical and World Myths.* New York: Oxford University Press.

Wasil, Rita. 1970. "Spanish Basque Folklore." University of Oregon Folklore Archives. Eugene, Oregon.

Webster, Richard, ed. [1911] 1950. *The Volume Library.* New York: Educators Association.

Weems, Mason L. [1809] 1976. *The Life of Washington,* ed. Marcus Cunliffe. Cambridge: The Belknap Press of Harvard University Press.

Four

Scholarship and Approaches

In the discussion of scholarship and approaches to folklore and story, it is important to remember that the vast amount of information covers many centuries and is international in scope. To begin to make an overview possible, this chapter is divided into two parts. Part 1 discusses the history, scholarship, and approaches taken in the study of folklore since the nineteenth century. Much of this record is available because of the American Folklore Society and careful records of its growth and interests since its founding in 1888. Part 2 is a discussion of story scholarship and approaches. Because of the revival in story-telling in the twentieth century and the increased recognition of the value of stories in both preserving traditions and shaping of everyday life, a number of texts have been written that represent perspectives of both the use of story and the new storytelling revival movements. Part 2 will draw from many of those sources to tell the story of story.

There are overlaps between Part 1 and part 2 because stories and narratives are often folklore themselves or, at the very least, enriched by folklore. Storytellers, either traditional (ethnic tellers of their own culture's orally transmitted lore) or nontraditional (tellers who borrow stories from around the world but who are not necessarily members of the culture they are sharing), use many kinds of oral prose to enhance and intrigue their listeners. Chapters 2 and 3 defined and gave many long and short examples of those prose narratives. It becomes obvious to the reader that there are many different kinds of folklore and story.

Folklorists are hesitant to use the term *genre* to define the different elements of their discipline because it is a literary term (meaning kinds or types of literature according to style, technique, or subject matter). Harmon and Holman's *A Handbook to Literature* (8th ed.) suggests that "Today a division of literature into *genres* would also include novel, short story, essay, television play, and motion picture scenario" (2000: 231). Even so, the term *genre* seems to work somewhat as a set of identifiers for the different types of folklore. In part 1, the different genres and folkloric scholarship fall into the important and previously emphasized categories of "oral," "material," "customary," and "belief," and within them are many subcategories. Within the studies of those basic categories there are multiple lenses or points of view that lead to various interpretations of the lore. Some folklorists are psychologically oriented, and those probe deeply into the symbolic meanings behind the lore. Oral-formulaic folklorists look for formulas and patterns in epic songs, ballads, and even sermons. Hemispheric folkloric studies examine relations between American folklore and American culture. Some folklorists look at the functionality or anthropology of the lore; that is, how does it work and why, what does it mean, and why does it last? Performance-oriented studies look at the way the lore is acted out or acted upon.

There are feminist perspectives that consider how women have contributed and have been acted upon by folkloric beliefs and behaviors over centuries of time. Further, some professional folklorists may have ideological points view that may reflect Marxist, capitalist, or other philosophical or social perspectives. There are folklorist who specialize in the studies of mass media and advertising, and public sector folklorists, who perform what is called applied folklore, who serve in schools, communities, and many kinds of museums. And, it should be stated that many folklorists are eclectic; that is, they have a variety of intermingled scholarly interests.

In part 2, the story and story telling genres will fall under the classifications of "traditional" and "nontraditional," and again, under those main headings, are many categories of scholarship perspectives and approaches. We will travel back in time and gain an introduction to a few of the earliest bards, many of whom were serious scholars of story, culture, and language. Skipping through the centuries and dipping into history here and there, the discussion will give examples of tellers and stories they told. We will reach the twentieth century, and that will bring us closer to today and the contemporary scholarship, approaches, and practice of professional and nonprofessional users of vernacular narratives and the myriad topics they describe.

PART 1: FOLKLORE SCHOLARSHIP AND APPROACHES

History

Expressive culture, that is the words, artifacts, behaviors, and beliefs that humans create and use evolve into definitions and markers that shape each culture. No two cultures or nationalities are the same, though there are often commonalities among them. Since the earliest days of conscious behaviors, human beings have wondered where they came from and how they got there. Studies and theories concerning how people arrived where they are, and what they kept from the past and what they largely discarded, have held fascination through the ages. America, that is, the United States, is a young country compared to many of the countries in the world. However, from the very beginning of the European encounter with the people of these Western continents of North, Central, and South America, there have been educated people curious enough to record and try to understand at least some of what they observed.

The actual study of American folklore may have begun as early as 1493 when Friar Ramon Pane came to the Americas with Christopher Columbus in order to study and collect the celebrations and artifacts of the American Taino Indians. That tribe and its expressive culture became the basis of *On the Antiquities of the Indians,* a book published by Pane in 1496. "In its emphasis upon the Indian and his quaintness, Pane's volume is typical of most of the works dealing with American folklore that followed it over the next four centuries" (McNeil 1996: 17). Unfortunately, the tribe is now extinct, as are many early American tribes, due to illness and extreme hardships that they could not endure.

W. K. McNeil, in his entry on "American Folklore Scholarship: The Early Years" in Jan Brunvand's *American Folklore: An Encyclopedia* (1996), informs us that Henry Rowe Schoolcraft (1793–1864) was the first American scholar to design a systematic format for a discipline of folklore. During Schoolcraft's lifetime, the word *folklore* was coined by the English scholar William J. Thoms, who defined it as *"the Lore of the People* ... [comprising] the manners, customs, observances, superstitions, ballads, proverbs, etc. of the olden time" (Brunvand 1996: 286). Schoolcraft, who was interested in cultural behaviors, created a discipline with four main points of interest: the physiology of man; material culture; intellectual and aesthetic interests, including music, poetry, oral tales and legends, medical information, and mythology; and the geographical influence on these topics of interest. This early scholar was more of a collector than theorist, but over time theoretical scholars published points of view relating to his topics of focus. Though it was not the same as folklore studies today, it was a beginning, and Schoolcraft is noted as the first of a long line of folklorists in the United States.

The primary focus of folklore collecting and study in the nineteenth century was American Indian lore, but as early as the 1830s, attention was beginning to appear concerning the African American slave songs. Three collectors,

William Francis Allen, Charles Pickard Ware, and Lucy McKim, published *Slave Songs of the United States* in 1867. That was early in the establishment of a genuine study of African American behaviors and lore, but it was a significant beginning. In 1880, Joel Chandler Harris produced the book *Uncle Remus: His Songs and His Sayings,* which was well received, and "there is little doubt that his various publications had a profound affect on the subsequent collecting of African American folktales" (McNeil 1996: 18).

The American Folklore Academy, with a mix of anthropologists, literary folklorists, and amateurs, was founded primarily by William Wells Newell with anthropologist Franz Boas. Samuel Clemens, better known as Mark Twain, and Joel Chandler Harris were both early members. Newell was deeply concerned about the professionalism of the society, and the new *Journal of American Folklore* was held to rigid scholarly standards. Newell leaned toward anthropological study because he recognized and respected Boas's methods of ethnographic field research. Boas "was concerned with an accurate recording of texts, and with an analysis of the texts either for linguistic purposes or for reconstruction of culture history through a study of the distribution of motifs" (Zumwalt 94: 1996). Their careful fieldwork has remained the basis for American folkloric studies.

Brunvand suggests that "The greatest divergence in the 20th century from the original concept of Thoms and his times concerning folklore has been to remove the emphasis on the rural and the past in order to include now as well the 'lore' of the modern, the urban, and the technologically advanced times" (1996: 286). The study of folklore, like other disciplines, has varied in its emphasis and style over the decades since its founding. There have been periods where the focus has been on behavioral or performance theories and practice; there have been influences from Marxism, feminism, modernism and postmodernism, and cultural studies. However, the study and preservation of the dynamics of expressed human behavior has always been at the core of this work, and professional folklorists continue to be respectful and sensitive to the sometimes delicate issues of representing others' beliefs, practices, behaviors, and traditions.

Scholarly Approaches

There are various ways to approach the study of folklore. The following few pages summarize various types of folklore analysis. Explanation and examples will be included to represent distinct areas of different theoretical points of view. Further reading in the various perspectives will increase understanding of the many ways folklore can be collected, classified, analyzed, and discussed, and names of well-known folklorists who work in the area of discussion are included in each section. Their work is readily available in the *Journal of American Folklore* and in texts they have written. Some of their primary works are listed in the bibliography at the end of this book.

Psychological

Because folklorists search for the meanings behind various types of folkloric practices and stories, and because they ask many questions about why people maintain certain traditions, beliefs, and behaviors, an understanding of psychology (the science of human behavior) plays a part in helping their investigations. Symbolism, the representation of ideas and things by the use of symbols, has been studied by many mythologists and psychologists, including Joseph Campbell, Carl Jung, and Sigmund Freud. Discussions of universal archetypes and collective human consciousness (universally shared images and thoughts), became important when related to folklore.

When a folklorist observes that children's storytelling and joking may have the same structure and function at similar ages and stages of development no matter where they are in the world, it begs to be examined. Folklorists with a feminist point of view are also interested in the psychology of folkloric behaviors in relation to masculinities and men's folklore. Some of the professional American folklorists who have done psychological studies are David Hufford, Alan Dundes, Jay Mechling, Gary Alan Fine, Carol Gilligan, and Elliot Oring.

Oral-Formulaic

Scholars who subscribe to this school examine the patterns and formulas in epic songs and poetry. Repetitive themes and groups of ideas repeat themselves in formulaic oral performance, and many disciplines (folklore, anthropology, and literature) have benefited from these studies. The knowledge gained has helped folklorists and linguists to understand the systems and formulas used in the recitation of long, epic songs and poetry. Lord Albert Bates and Milman Parry were forerunners in this study, and John Miles Foley, a scholar of orally performed poetry and other formulaic forms, has been active in continuing research and publishing valuable information in this genre.

Historic-Geographic

This approach to folklore studies is comparative, that is, the researcher compares different versions or variants of the same story, artifact, custom, or belief. Often called the "Finnish method," the method was based on the early work of Elias Lönnrot, a Finn who gathered information from songs and ballads and then created a sequential narrative of the Finnish epic, *The Kalevala*. His method intrigued Finnish folklorists Julius Krohn (1835–88), Kaarle Krohn (1863–1933), and Antti Aarne (1867–1925), and they formulated a system to track the historical continuity of an item. These scholars would gather every version of a story they could find and then try to determine where the story started and how it had been spread or disseminated.

> Julius' son Kaarle Krohn set out to test the idea that European folktales came from India in historical times by reconstructing the original forms of individual tales and, at the same time, determining their original homes and their paths of migration. His method was called historic-geographic because early (literary) variants are arranged historically and later (oral) variants are grouped geographically, in order to achieve the reconstruction as objectively as possible. (Goldberg 1996: 152)

Archer Taylor (1890–1973) and Stith Thompson (1885–1976) brought the method to folklorists in the United States. The American approach has been less exacting, but the historic-geographic comparative methods have been used to study ballad and proverb collections as well as riddles, material artifacts, and particularly in the study of the origins of African folktales. In the mid-twentieth century in the United States, this complex approach became less popular. In studies of widely disseminated oral lore such as jokes, legends, and even regional slang, the origins simply could not be located and compared with any plausibility. Even so, the method is important because it provides a way to compare common practices, beliefs, and traditions in very disparate cultures. As Goldberg stated, "With it, folklorists can explore both the unity and the diversity of mankind" (153).

Hemispheric

Richard Dorson (1916–1981) believed that American folklore, American studies, culture, and history were strongly connected. He called this interdisciplinary linking the hemispheric approach. Dorson, through teaching, writing, and building the folklore program at Indiana University at Bloomington, Indiana, is largely credited with building folklore as a serious academic study in the United States. "Dorson insisted that a folklorist should be broadly trained in comparative studies but should know at least one culture in depth" (Baker 1998: 162). He was also keenly interested in the way authors used folklore in literature, and he wrote that identifying folklore in literature was only the beginning of critical literary interpretation. Dorson taught that finding evidence of folklore of different types of literary work demonstrated the author's knowledge, but it only began to raise questions as to how and why it was used, where it came from, and how the author may have come to know it.

Functional or Anthropological

This approach is based on the meanings and functions of folklore in traditional behaviors and communication between people. A style often used by scholars with training in sociology, history, and other social sciences, William Bascom (1912–81) suggested that folklorists would benefit by examining four functions or performances that folklore contributed to the ongoing interactions of society. The four functions he designated were first *escape,* meaning that the practice of fantasy, either imaginary or acted out, could assist an individual to turn away from the frustrations and restrictions of everyday society. Secondly, he designated *validation,* meaning that folklore or traditional behavior of a group could be validated by its rituals and established ways of doing things. Third, Bascom suggested that folklore provides cultural and societal *education* in a group or community. It is through folkloric practice that the values of a society are passed on to the next generation. The fourth function, Bascom stated, was *social control.* Folklore can be used as a method to ensure conformity by using rewards for conformity and punishment for nonconformity (Bascom 1954: 333–49).

Other folklorists who taught and practiced a functional perspective (in addition to other perspectives) were and are the late Alan Dundes (1934–2005), Elliott Oring, Tom Burns, Barre Toelken, and Patrick B. Mullen.

Performance

Folklorist Richard Bauman is one of the best known scholars in the study of performance-oriented folklore. His focus is on the act of storytelling, not simply the text itself. He pays close attention to the interrelationships between the way telling is accomplished, and the links between the form of the story and the function of the story in the culture. Bauman's book *Story, Performance, and Event: Contextual Studies of Oral Narrative* (1993) is an important source of orally performed narratives. Barre Toelken, a scholar of Navajo folkways and folklife, has discussed the elements of story performance and audience among traditional Navajo tellers. Toelken's 1969 essay "The 'Pretty

Pueblo storytelling figures from the Southwest United States. *The Four Winds Gallery, Pittsburgh, PA.*

Language' of Yellowman," offers a close analysis of the interactions between the performance of a Navajo teller and his audience.

Feminist

Since the 1970s, feminism has been a strong voice in American folklore. Male bias was present in much of the earlier scholarship, and publications of women folklorists have brought a clearer picture to students, scholars, and general readership of the importance of women in tradition bearing, culture, and practice. Discussions over the following decades identified the separation between designated public and private spheres for men and women, and discussions addressed ubiquitous power relations between the sexes. One of the earliest voices was that of Clair R. Farrar, and in decades that followed, Rosan A. Jordan, Susan J. Kalčik, Joan Newlon Radner, Polly Stewart, Camilla A. Collins, Margaret A. Mills, and others have contributed to exposing entrenched negative cultural constructions and distortions in the way women have been represented (or not represented) in folkloric and cultural studies. Feminist folklorists continue to work at defining women in relationship to other men and women, exploring creative ways women have responded to negation and marginalization, and looking for answers to the ubiquitous question "So what?".

Ideological

Examining patterns of Marxist, capitalist, Christian, and other social and political systems has not engaged many scholars in the United States. Folk literature and folk music, often representing oppressed classes, has interested a handful of folklorists in the United States, including Charles Seeger, Carl Boggs, and Tim Patterson. Concerns about the folklore of capitalism, that is the consumer society, led George Lipsitz to write *Class and Culture in Cold War America: "A Rainbow at Midnight"* in 1981. Studies of Christian folk religion in the United States range from the study of revival customs in the American Bible Belt to rattlesnake worship in the hills of Kentucky, Virginia, and Tennessee (Roberts 1990: 229).

Mass-Cultural

With the rise of the Internet, Web sites, e-mail, and other electronic communications devices, along with television and films, a quick dissemination of rumor, legend, jokes, and narratives has become common. Scholars studying these phenomena are myriad. Linda Dégh wrote a text called *American Folklore and the Mass Media* (1994), and other scholars in the American Folklore Academy including Bill Ellis, Carl Lindahl, and Jan Brunvand have focused on the diffusion of narratives through various venues of mass culture.

Public Sector

Public sector folklorists work primarily to inform and educate the public about the importance of expressive and traditional culture, and they work in many preservation efforts. Their work may be in various types of museums, libraries, cultural centers, and schools. The American Folklife Center at the

Library of Congress, directed by folklorist Peggy Bulger, is an example of archival resources that many universities emulate. Paddy Bowman, director of the National Network for Folk Arts in Education, is another catalyst in the public sector of American folklore. Bowman maintains a wide network of Internet connections and information, available to anyone interested in accessing it, for United States educators and students in every state. The public sector folklorists play an important role in sustaining, maintaining, and encouraging folkloric creativity throughout all socioeconomic classes and ethnic or religious groups. They might be called the effective cheerleaders for folklore in America.

Genres and Scholars

The following are genre definitions and an overview of scholars working in each area. These descriptions present but a sampling of the thousands of topics scholars and students pursue in engagement with folkloric study and are representative of topics presented at recent (2000–2005) folklore conferences, and therefore indicate areas of interest to contemporary folklore field workers and scholars.

Oral Folklore

Oral folklore is vernacular, that is, it is transmitted by word-of mouth. Much of it has been collected, classified, analyzed, written, discussed and archived in the last few centuries.

Myth   The most famous mythologist of the twentieth century was Joseph Campbell (1904–1987), though he was certainly not alone in his serious pursuit of the meaning and power of mythology in shaping the cultural folkways and mores of the world. Campbell was particularly interested in the hero and the hero cycle, but others, such as Lord Raglan (1788–1855), Sigmund Freud (1856–1939), Otto Rank (1884–1939), and Carl Jung (1875–1961), the latter two both students of Freud, were the inspiration and forerunners of Campbell's famous work. Campbell wrote and taught for four decades, and his most famous book was *The Hero with a Thousand Faces* (1968). Seeking to understand the human mind and its relationships with nature, other humans, and self, Campbell and mythologists like him delve deeply into the psychological workings of the human mind. Why do we do what we do? How much are we shaped by imagination? How does our language reflect who we are? How do we know which stories to keep, and which to discard? What was the beginning, and will there be an end? Is there another dimension to living, one we can sense but not see? These are the questions, and many more, that mythologists ask and pursue.

Legend   The most important work done in the study of legends currently is being performed by Jan Brunvand, Linda Dégh, Bill Ellis, and Veronique Campion-Vincent. Brunvand, a retired folklorist who taught for many years in the English department at the University of Utah in Salt Lake City, continues to publish books addressing the urban legend. One of his latest collections, *Be Afraid, Be Very Afraid: The Book of Scary Urban Legends* (2004), was gathered in part from readers of his earlier published collections or of his syndicated newspaper collections. Brunvand suggests that "While these stories are not literally true, any more than a horror film is, when hearing them we realize that they *could* be true" (Brunvand 2004: 13). He has maintained that the stories, with unidentifiable sources other than friend-of-a-friend, are manifestations of anxiety in society. Stories about children being quickly disguised and abducted from huge stores like Wal-Mart and Target, or about alligators in urban sewers or young women being killed (cooked inside) by too much time in tanning beds circulate within society and are often passed along as true.

Linda Dégh, a retired professor from Indiana University, also continues to research and publish on legend topics. One of her recent books, *Legend and Belief: Dialectics of a Folklore Genre* (2002), has been very useful in graduate folklore classes. The discussion ranges from a variety of definitions for legend to legend-tellers. She is now working on another book about folklore and legends aimed at younger readers. Folklorist Bill Ellis (Pennsylvania State University) and Veronique Campion-Vincent (Maison des Science de l'Homme) recently presented their current research on transnational conspiracy theories at the American Folklore Society conference (October, 2005). Ellis has published several books on legends that we live in terms of the supernatural, and Campion-Vincent's book on urban legends in France will be published early in 2006.

Folktale   One of the most well known and prolific scholars and writers of literary folklore was Zora Neale Hurston (1891–1960). Born in the first incorporated, all-black town in the United States, Eatonville, Florida, her father (John Hurston) served three times as the mayor of this self-governing town. As a Baptist preacher, he was a man of words, and Zora Neale Hurston became well-educated through her own industry and curiosity. Hurston was a part of the Harlem Renaissance in the 1920s, a time of the blossoming of African American art, literature, and music, and she was a skilled folklorist, anthropologist, and ethnographer. She traveled throughout Florida and

Louisiana, gathering folklore, and then wrote many volumes of fiction incorporating the folklore into engaging stories: *Jonah's Gourd Vine* (1934), *Mules and Men* (1935), *Their Eyes Were Watching God* (1937), *Tell My Horse* (1938), *Moses, Man of the Mountain* (1939), *Dust Tracks on a Road* (1942), and *Seraph on the Suwanee* (1948).

The research in folktale and fairy tales by Max Lüthi (1909–) and Francis Lee Utley (1907–1974) continues to be greatly valued and used by academic folklorists both in the United States and in Europe. Lüthi's text *Once upon A Time: On the Nature of Fairy Tales* (1976) remains as a definitive discussion of the underlying meaning and context of many folk and fairy tales, and it is often quoted in other scholars' work. Utley's *The Study of Folk Literature: Its Scope and Use* (1958), published by the American Folklore Society, also continues to be an important discussion concerning the presence of folktales and their use in literature.

Folklorist Sandra Dolby Stahl wrote an important book in the study of folktale and personal narrative. *Literary Folkloristics and the Personal Narrative* (1989) discusses literary folkloristics, the personal narrative as an oral literary genre, and interpreting personal narrative texts and includes analytical examples that demonstrate the selection process of a narrator during a verbal performance. Dolby Stahl suggests that "By identifying tradition in a given listener's interpretive context, the scholar creates an instructional text, which in turn allows the process of interpretation itself to be examined" (Dolby Stahl 1989: 119).

Though the work of some of the scholars mentioned is not recent, it is still considered seminal (primary and critical) work and influences the work of today's students and scholars of folkloristics. As the discipline of folklore unfolded in the late nineteenth and early twentieth centuries, insights and understandings were expressed and built upon by one scholar after another. The work of the early folklore researchers, as well as the work of students, past and present, is valued and incorporated into the study of folktale and other genres within the discipline.

Fairy Tale   A profusion of texts and articles about fairy tales have come forth in the second half of twentieth century. Well-known folklorists, literary specialists, and cultural studies researchers have informed scholars and the public readership of the history and origin of many well-known fairy tales. The discussions range from how the tales reflected lived society and culture, to adaptations for the Italian and French court, to feminist discussion of male oppression and domination present in many of the traditional tales. The Walt Disney studios, as mentioned above, have adapted many tales and produced films for family entertainment. However, many of the tales have complex histories, and there are variants of most of the tales, about which the American public is seldom informed.

Folklorist Jack Zipes, editor of *The Great Fairy Tale Tradition* (2001), states that: "In fact, the literary fairy tale has evolved from the stories of the oral tradition, piece by piece, in a process of incremental adaptation, generation by generation in the different cultures of the people who cross-fertilized the oral tales and disseminated them" (2001: xi). Zipes's text (and many others) includes fairytales versions from Gianfrancesco Straparola, Jacob and Wilhelm Grimm, Giambattista Basile, Charles Perrault, Marie-Catherine d'Aulnoy, and many others representing versions of the tales from many different countries and cultures.

The late Alan Dundes, one of the most well known folklorists in the United States, wrote informed texts and edited anthologies on many topics in folklore. "Casebooks," as he called many of them, on "Cinderella," "Little Red Riding Hood," vampires, urban lore, photocopier lore, and other topics, including introductory folklore books, represent his scholarship and dedication to the dynamic world of folk and fairy tale. His work will stand for decades as having provided both exemplary scholarship and information.

Marina Warner is a cultural critic rather than a folklorist, but her scholarly voice has been strong and beneficial in the genres of folk and fairytale. Warner lives in London and is the author of four novels and many works of nonfiction. Warner's *From the Beast to the Blond: On Fairy Tales and Their Tellers* (1994) is a landmark study of the long history and embedded meanings in fairy tales. She suggests, with clearly discussed evidence to back up her hypothesis, that the realistic themes in famous folk and fairytales are skillful methods that adults use to convey advice, warning, and even hope to children and to adults. Robert Darnton, a professor of history at Princeton University, is also a cultural critic. His important text, *The Great Cat Massacre and Other Episodes in French Cultural History* (1985), includes a chapter titled "Peasants Tell Tales: The Meaning of Mother Goose." In it, the reader gains further enlightenment about the origin, meaning, and use of common fairytales. Darnton states:

> The peasants of early modern France inhabited a world of step-mothers and orphans, of inexorable, unending toil, and of brutal emotions, both raw and repressed. The human condition has changed so much since then that we can hardly imagine the way it appeared to people whose lives were really nasty, brutish, and short. That is why we need to reread Mother Goose. . . . Consider four of the best-known stories from Perrault's Mother Goose—"Puss'n Boots," "Tom

Thumb," "Cinderella," and "The Ridiculous Wishes" in comparison with some of the peasant tales that treat the same themes. (Darnton 1985: 29)

Material Folklore Studies

Material folkloric studies are often defined as the study of things people make with their hands. The following genres represent only a small portion of folkloric items that fit into this category, but they are significant topics of scholarship in the study of material folklore.

Folk Art   The definition of folk art is fluid. Most often it is art that is learned in nonacademic settings, and it is an art that is often transmitted by word of mouth and from generation to generation. Many types of art fall under this broad heading, and it includes objects from ethnic groups and tourist artifacts to fine art. Even the popular art of mass culture sometimes falls into the category of folk art. This is art often used in everyday life, and it serves both as a reminder of heritage and respect and as a continuity with the past. Several prominent folklorists have contributed to the scholarship and preservation of American and international folk art.

Henry Glassie wrote *The Spirit of Folk Art* (1995), *The Potter's Art* (1999), and *Material Culture* (1999), and all include representations and critical discussion about the folk arts of many countries. John Michael Vlach and Simon J. Bronner edited a collection of folk art discussions called *Folk Art and Art Worlds* (1992), which primarily discusses different types of American folk art over time and place.

One more text that will enhance the readers' knowledge is *American Folk* (2001). Written by a group of curators from the Museum of Fine Arts, Boston (Ward et al.), the text has a particularly lucid discussion of what folk art is, and isn't: "Broadly speaking, folk art is an umbrella term that covers many types of artistic expressions, once often called 'primitive,' 'rustic,' or 'naïve,' but now more likely to be referred to as nonacademic, amateur, self-taught, popular, provincial, rural, vernacular, or (in the case of twentieth-century work) outsider" (9).

Foodlore   The study of food, its meanings, and its ever-changing dynamics have been of interest to folklorists for decades. Both everyday life and customary celebrations involve a variety of food traditions in every culture. Folklorists have begun to delve more deeply into the meanings behind foodway traditions, searching for ways the concepts of folklore can help to clarify their understanding of food traditions. Lucy Long, a folklore professor at Bowling Green State University, has done significant research and publishing in foods and folklore, including her edited anthology *Culinary Tourism* (2004). Jill Rudy, Rachel H. Saltzman, Jacqueline Thursby, and many other folklorists are teaching, researching, and publishing in this genre.

Cemetery Studies   Gravestones and their symbolic meanings, such as crosses for Christians, six-pointed stars for Jews, the yin-yang symbol for Buddhists, lambs for innocence, hearts for love, and angels for protection, have drawn folklorists and other curious onlookers since formal cemeteries were begun in the United States in the mid-1800s. There are growing numbers of folklorists engaged in serious preservation efforts, photography, classification, analysis, and discussion of the cemeteries of the world.

An ancient Celtic grave marker with a mixture of symbolic designs.

These cities of the dead, or necropolises, are representations of art, architecture, ethnicity, regionalism, economics, and other elements of culture. Richard Meyer, J. Joseph Edgette, Tom and Brenda Malloy, Gary Collison, David Mayer Gradwohl, and others have worked tirelessly for decades to build an academic presence in this important genre. *Markers,* an academic journal edited by Gary Collison, is sponsored by the Association for Gravestone Studies based in Greenfield, Massachusetts. Meyer has published two books on the topic: *Cemeteries and Gravemarkers: Voices of American Culture* (1992) and *Ethnicity and the American Cemetery* (1993).

Customary Folklore

Customary celebrations are traditional performances that often occur regularly through the calendar year. In the United States, holidays such as Thanksgiving, Christmas, and the Fourth of July (among others) mean a few days off of work or school and usually a party of one kind or another. There are religious celebrations, presidents' days, and a myriad of birthdays, anniversaries, and other occasions for family dinners and acknowledgment. Traditional dancing, often ethnic, and many kinds of music are also topics studied by various folklorists.

Folk Celebrations: Regional and National   Customary calendar celebrations around the world have drawn folkloric interest throughout the history of the discipline. From the Festival of San Fermin and the running of the bulls in Pamplona, Spain, to the Veiled Prophet Ball and Parade in St. Louis, to the Mardi Gras in New Orleans and the "other" Mardi Gras (a family version) in Mobile, Alabama, folklorists are drawn to and participate in the festival celebrations of the world. There are calendar customs such as Valentine's Day, the Fourth of July in the United States, Boxing Day in England, and countless other festival days in India, China, Japan, and other countries. The list is endless, and so is the energy of folklorists who pursue the meanings, stories, and varied traditions of these often colorful affairs.

Victor Turner, who edited the text *Celebration: Studies in Festivity and Ritual* (1984), contributed greatly to the studies of the symbolic meanings of folk festival. Alessandro Falassi, who edited the text *Time out of Time: Essays on the Festival* (1987) expanded festival studies by including articles on festivals from Europe, North and South America, Africa, Asia, and Oceana. Both of these books introduce the teacher and the student to cultural celebrations from around the world. Turner's book was published to coincide with a major international exhibition at the Smithsonian Institution. The essays in Falassi's collection take the reader to Europe, North and South America, Africa, Asia, and Oceania. Both Turner and Falassi were academic anthropologists who understood well the critical intersections of anthropology and folklore, both disciplines that require deep probing into the meanings behind the playing out of traditional culture.

Jack Santino, a folklorist at Bowling Green State University, has, among many other folkloric interests, focused on the celebrations of Halloween. In *Halloween and Other Festivals of Death and Life* (2000), he has included essays that reflect on the celebration and meanings of Halloween from a variety of perspectives. The varied essays take us to Halloween celebrations in Scotland, Newfoundland, the Texas-Mexico region, Canada, Vermont, and the American South. In *The Hallowed Eve: Dimensions of Culture in a Calendar Festival in Northern Ireland,* Santino explicates the meaning of the "Irish Christmas."

Folk Dance   From the Charleston to the jitterbug and moving on to rap, customs of folk dance have been little studied in a systematic way by American folklorists. In a country where so many nationalities have learned to share one another's traditions and customary expressions, it is surprising that, overall, so little has been done to document and preserve the dance traditions. With the improvement in documentation techniques, more studies have been undertaken, but there are many that need to be accomplished.

Contemporary intertribal Native American social dances, called Powwow, have been studied by several folklorist including Vanessa Brown and Barre Toelken ("American Indian Powwow," [1988]), and in another study published by Toelken ("Ethnic Selection and Intensification in the Native American Powwow," [1991]). A few more recent studies of American folk dance are: LeeEllen Freidland's "Social Commentary in African American Movement Performance" (1995), Dorothea Hast's "Performance, Transformation, and Community: Contra Dance in New England" (1993), Colin Quigley's "A Hearing to Designate the Square Dance the American Folk Dance of the United States: Cultural Politics and an American Vernacular Dance Form" (1994), and Sylvia Rodriguez' "Defended Boundaries, Precarious Elites: The Arroyo Seco Matachines Dance" (1994).

Folk Music   From the bluegrass music of Appalachia to the blues that swing from New Orleans to Chicago and points east and west, folk music permeates the United States. Soulful ballads and upbeat lyrics hum on CD's, the Internet, and even old-fashioned radios carry thousands of folk tunes, both contemporary and from the long-ago past. Concerts of every kind, from ragtime to heavy metal, are easy to find, and folklorists enjoy the beat and rhythms of the music. The folkloric study of grassroots music in the United States is huge. William Ferris wrote *Blues from the Delta* in 1978; Bill C. Malone wrote *Singing Cowboys and Musical Mountaineers: Southern Culture and the Roots of Country Music* in 1993; and there are books about ballads, British folksongs (Tristram Potter Coffin's *The British Traditional Ballad in North America,* 1977) adapted in America, and more. The list goes one and on. The most efficient way to find the scholars in this vast realm may be to choose a type of folk music that you are seeking to study and turn to a good folklife or folklore encyclopedia to find the scholars publishing in your particular area of interest.

Folklore of Belief

Human beings, with limitless imaginations and perceived needs, create and construct many belief systems. There is an overlap in the oral expressions among folk superstitions, folk religion, and folk medicine. The boundaries of superstition, folk religion, and even folk medicine are fuzzy, but all are traditional oral behaviors passed from person to person, and which consistently carry meaning for the participants.

Folk Religion and the Supernatural   In 1982, David J. Hufford wrote a book called *The Terror That Comes in the Night: An Experience-Centered Study of Supernatural Assault Traditions.* Stories of the phenomenon of "The Old Hag" (a type of paralysis or impression that someone or something is sitting on one's chest in the dark of the night) and other equally frightening and inexplicable nightmares fill this fascinating book. To date, there has not been another book published like this one. Hufford is an interdisciplinary folklorist, and he is one of the few folklorists who work on the folkloric dimension of medical beliefs and practices.

Folk Medicine   The practice of folk medicine is based on oral transmission of remedies and cures rather than formal academic or clinical training of the practitioners. Herbalism is one of the most popular forms of American folk medicine, and other forms of home remedies, naturopathic healing, and magic are all subsumed under this heading. Common cause-and-effect beliefs, such as touching a toad being a cause of warts, or throwing the hands to the face in fright while pregnant will causing a significant birthmark on the infant's face, are both oral folk superstitions and folk belief.

Hufford wrote an essay called "Folk Healers" in 1983, and in it he pointed out some interesting and important separations between American folkloric medical practice and academic medicine. He stated:

The connections of a folk healing tradition with its cultural context are also important for understanding healers and their patients. A tendency to focus on individual traditions as being discrete and self-contained has resulted in part from too great a dependence on modern academic medicine as a model for analysis. In recent centuries Western academic medicine has undergone a more or less intentional process of separation from other facets of culture. This separateness, though still more apparent than real, appears very unusual when compared with the situation in other cultures, where health systems are strongly related to such other aspects of culture as religion and artistic expression. (Hufford 1983: 308)

Another interesting aspect of folk medicine is the practice of the *curanderos,* or folk healers in the Mexican-American community. Folklore scholars who have made a study of these practitioners are Joe S. Graham, who wrote "Folk Medicine and Intracultural Diversity among West Texas Mexican Americans" (1985), and Robert T. Trotter II and Juan A. Chavira, who wrote the text *Curanderismo* (1981).

Education and Folklore

Paddy Bowman, Jan Rosenberg, and Susan Eleuterio, all professional folklorists and teachers, have worked tirelessly to provide folklore resources for K–12 teachers throughout the United States. Bowman is the director of the National Network for Folk Arts in Education, Rosenberg is connected with Heritage Education Resources, Inc., and Eleuterio with GRANTS, Inc. These women, and other members of the Folklore and Education Section of the American Folklore Society, sponsored the Twelfth Annual Folklore and Education Workshop, which has been held in conjunction with the American Folklore Society conference. This provides K–12 teachers from the region in which the conference is held to learn about researching, documenting, and writing about community and folk culture. In 2005, the workshop emphasized the teaching of literacy, and participants included folklorists, teachers, and students.

PART 2: STORY SCHOLARSHIP AND APPROACHES

History, Scholars, and Scribes

Burning Brightly: New Light on Old Tales Told Today (1998), by Kay Stone, is the first book-length discussion of the genre of professional storytelling in the United States. As explained by the text, for some years there has been a major storytelling revival throughout the American continent, and hundreds of local groups, storytelling communities, centers, clubs, and national conferences have been organized. Since the late nineteenth century, storytelling has been an important part of professional training for librarians, and university programs are now including classes in storytelling in drama departments in response to public demand. Stone's book explores storytelling through the voices of the storytellers themselves. "Issues such as the modern recontexualization of old tales and the role of women in folktales are linked to individual storytelling accounts. Texts of eight stories that exemplify the approaches of the various storytellers are also included" (Stone 1998: back cover).

Joseph Daniel Sobol, a folklorist and professor at East Tennessee State University, wrote *The Storytellers' Journey: An American Revival* (1999). The book is a history of the last 30 years of American storytelling, but it also offers an in-depth exploration of the psychological roots of the storytelling revival and the consistent power of the talented storyteller. Suggesting that the storytelling revival is reflective of a larger process of cultural revitalization in the United States, Sobol traces the growth of the National Association for the Preservation and Perpetuation of Storytelling (NAPPS), in Jonesborough, Tennessee, and details the passions, politics, and social and mythic forces that have contributed to the structure of this national and international network of arts professionals.

Sobol is also coeditor (with John Gentile) of *Storytelling, Self, and Society: An Interdisciplinary Journal of Storytelling Stories.* The first volume was released in the fall of 2004 and includes essays by well-known folklore scholars and storytellers. Among the contributors to the first issue were Jo Radner, David Novak, Karen Dietz, Gioia Timpanelli, and Doug Lipman, all well known for their former contributions to building this growing genre. John Miles Foley, who wrote *How to Read and Oral Poem* (2002), contributed an article titled "From Performance to Paper to the Web: New Ways of (Re-) Presenting Told Stories." The journal promises to be an excellent source of up-to-date information about the field.

Another helpful book is Anne Pellowski's text *The World of Storytelling* (1977). A professional librarian at the New York Public Library and formerly director librarian at the Information Center on Children's Cultures, U.S. Committee for UNICEF, Pellowski is one of America's foremost authorities on storytelling around the world. The text describes the history and definition of storytelling, ranges through various types, discusses the format and style of storytelling, and also explains the training of storytellers. Though the book is not new, it is exceptionally informative and contains information that simply does not become dated.

The Storyteller and the Craft

Ruth Stotter, folklorist, storyteller, and founder of the Dominican College Storytelling Program at San Rafael, California, has published several texts about story and storytelling. In *About Story: Writings on Stories and Storytelling 1980–1994* (1996), she shares scholarship, psychological insights, techniques, and many creative ideas for storytelling. *The Golden Axe and other Folktales of Compassion and Greed* (1998) includes a collection of stories from around the world that demonstrate the role culture plays in the shaping of vernacular narratives. A text useful to teachers and students, Stotter has also included the Stith Thompson tale types and motifs so that the tales can easily be used for comparative study. The identifications of tales "allows scholars to identify, classify, and locate stories with similar formats" (Stotter 1998: 8). In *More about Story: Writings on Stories and Storytelling 1995–2001* (2002), Stotter leads the reader through a world of "Story Application: A–Z." Tips ranging from "Attitude" to "Ending the Story" are included in this useful guide.

Doug Lipman, a storyteller, musician, Parents' Choice Award–winning recording artist, and storytelling coach and instructor, tells us that in his text, *Improving Your Storytelling: Beyond the Basics for All Who Tell Stories in Work or Play* (1999), the reader will find strategies and frameworks that go beyond the basics and assist the teller to make quick and informed decisions while storytelling. In discussion that ranges from basics to the forms of imagery and their effects on listeners, Lipman, in an exceptionally accessible style, takes the reader through a process of self-development in the art of storytelling. He suggests "whys" and "why nots" to better communicate the art of storytelling to his readers.

Three additional books that should be considered for this section are Marni Gillard's *Storyteller, Story Teacher: Discovering the Power of Storytelling for Teaching and Living* (1996); Joseph Sobol's *The House between Earth and Sky: Harvesting New American Folktales* (2005); and *The Storyteller's Guide: Storytellers Share Advice for the Classroom, Boardroom, Showroom, Podium, Pulpit, and Center Stage* (1996), written and edited by Bill Mooney and David Holt.

Gillard, a teacher and professor of language arts and reading methods at Russell Sage College, takes us to a different dimension of storytelling. Family stories, conversational anecdotes, polished nontraditional performances tales, oral history, and even songs and poems are discussed and validated as natural stories to be shared and enjoyed. Sobol's text shares multicultural and multilingual proverbs, beliefs, remedies, recipes, and folktales authentically collected from English as a Second Language (ESL) students Sobol taught in four Chicago schools. The text contains resources, teaching strategies, and step-by-step guides for story collecting. Mooney and Holt, professional actors and narrators, have put together a text with anecdotes, metaphors, and parables gathered from more than 50 storytellers, "including teachers, librarians, authors, musicians, actors, clergymen, and full time professionals" (Mooney and Holt 1996: back cover). The text is lively and will engage readers in an entertaining way as a peek into the learning experiences of practicing storytellers.

Approaches for Engagement with the Tales

Engaging teachers and students with folktales, fairy tales, mythology, and simply the lore of everyday stories requires context, examples, and a comfortable learning climate. The following books can be used for engagement with the tales, and there is enough variety to meet the need of teachers and students who would like short tales or extended narratives. Many of these are not "hot-off-the-press," but they are respected in professional teaching of folklore and stories and contain a wealth of useful information and examples.

In *New Tales for Old: Folktales as Literary Fictions for Young Adults* (1999), Gail de Vos and Anna E. Altmann, professional university instructors and storytellers, share substantial information about folktales and literary fictions. Using tale-type indexing, variants of classic tales are shared and made applicable through materials for classroom extension. Rich bibliographies are included with each tale, and it is an accessible and enjoyable text for teachers, professors, and students at both the high school and university level. *Tell Me a Fairy Tale: A Parent's Guide to Telling Magical and Mythical Stories* (1995) by Bill Adler, Jr., is both informative and funny. Appropriate for classroom use as well as family adaptation, the text offers synopses of tales and suggestions for making the tales less stereotyped and sexist. It is creative, and students enjoy it.

Folklorist Archer Taylor (1890–1973) wrote *The Proverb and an Index to "The Proverb"* originally in 1931 (Cambridge/Mass). Another deeply respected academic folklorist, Wolfgang Mieder, wrote an introduction and bibliography for a newly released edition (1985). The book contains a treasure-trove of long and short proverbs, their origins, and their classifications. It is usable, accessible, and interesting in terms of its multicultural range. Another text, *Untying the Knot: On Riddles and Other Enigmatic Modes* (1996) is useful in the classroom for reference and sources for telling. Galit Hasan-Rokem and David

Shulman, editors, have gathered essays that speak to a profound number of riddles, enigmatic modes, and antiquarian myths from around the world.

Three last books, mentioned because of the wealth of amusing and informative stories within them, are *Irish Wake Amusements* (1967) by Seán O Súilleabháin (available used); *Folktales of England* (1965) by Katherine M. Briggs and Ruth L. Tongue; and *Storytellers, Saints, and Scoundrels: Folk Narrative in Hindu Religious Teaching* (1989) by Kirin Narayan. Beyond the obvious multicultural dimension of these three texts, the discussions of listener orientations, contextual background, and broadly informing prefaces and introductions help the reader to approach the world of storytelling with a richly informed and prepared perspective. They are all three easily accessible and very useful.

WORKS CITED

Adler, Bill, Jr. 1995. *Tell Me a Fairy Tale: A Parent's Guide to Telling Magical and Mythical Stories.* New York: Penguin Books.

Baker, Ronald L. 1998. "Richard M. Dorson." In *Encyclopedia of Folklore and Literature,* ed. Mary Ellen Brown and Bruce A. Rosenberg. Santa Barbara, CA: ABC-CLIO.

Bascom, William R. 1954. "Four Functions of Folklore." *Journal of American Folklore* 67: 333–349.

Bauman, Richard. 1993. *Story, Performance, and Event: Contextual Studies of Oral Narrative.* Cambridge: Cambridge University Press.

Briggs, Katherine M., and Ruth L. Tongue. 1965. *Folktales of England.* Chicago: University of Chicago Press.

Brown, Vanessa, and Barre Toelken. 1988. "American Indian Powwow." *Folklife Annual 1987,* 46–68. Washington, DC: American Folklife Center.

Brunvand, Jan Harold, ed. 1996. *American Folklore: An Encyclopedia.* New York: Garland.

———. 2004. *Be Afraid, Be Very Afraid: The Book of Scary Urban Legends.* New York: W.W. Norton.

Campbell, Joseph. 1968. *The Hero with a Thousand Faces.* Princeton: Princeton University Press.

Coffin, Tristram Potter. 1977. *The British Traditional Ballad in North America.* Rev. ed. with a supplement by Roger DeV. Renwick. Austin: University of Texas Press.

Darnton, Robert. 1984. *The Great Cat Massacre and Other Episodes in French Cultural History.* New York: Vintage Books.

Dégh, Linda. 2001. *Legend and Belief: Dialectics of a Folklore Genre.* Bloomington: Indiana University Press.

———. 1994. *American Folklore and the Mass Media.* Bloomington: Indiana University Press.

de Vos, Gail, and Anna E. Altmann. 1999. *New Tales for Old: Folktales as Literary Fictions for Young Adults.* Englewood, CO: Libraries Unlimited.

Dolby Stahl, Sandra. 1989. *Literary Folkloristics and the Personal Narrative.* Bloomington: Indiana University Press.

Dundes, Alan, ed. 1982. *Cinderella: A Casebook.* Madison: University of Wisconsin Press.

Falassi, Alessandro, ed. 1987. *Time out of Time: Essays on the Festival.* Albuquerque: University of New Mexico Press.

Ferris, William. 1978. *Blues from the Delta.* Garden City, NY. Anchor Publishing.

Foley, John Miles. 2002. *How to Read an Oral Poem.* Urbana: University of Illinois Press.

———. 2004. "From Performance to Paper to the Web: New Ways of (Re-) Presenting Told Stories." *Storytelling, Self, Society: An Interdisciplinary Journal of Storytelling Studies* 1(1): 92–108.

Friedland, LeeEllen. 1995. "Social Commentary in African American Movement Performance." In *Human Action Signs in Cultural Context: The Visible and the Invisible in Movement and Dance,* ed. Brenda Farnell, 136–57. Metuchen, NJ: Scarecrow.

Gillard, Marni. 1996. *Storyteller, Story Teacher: Discovering the Power of Storytelling for Teaching and Living.* Portland, ME: Stenhouse Publishers.

Glassie, Henry. 1995. *The Spirit of Folk Art: The Girard Collection at the Museum of International Folk Art.* New York: Harry N. Abrams.

———. 1999. *The Potter's Art: Material Culture.* Bloomington: Indiana University Press.

———. 1999. *Material Culture.* Bloomington: Indiana University Press.

Goldberg, Christine. 1996. "Comparative Approach." In *American Folklore: An Encyclopedia,* ed. Jan Harold Brunvand, 151–54. New York: Garland.

Graham, Joe S. 1985. "Folk Medicine and Intracultural Diversity among West Texas Mexican Americans." *Western Folklore* 44: 168–193.

Harmon, William, and C. Hugh Holman. 2000. *A Handbook to Literature.* 8th ed. Upper Saddle River, NJ: Prentice Hall.

Hasan-Rokem, Galit, and David Shulman, eds. 1966. *Untying the Knot: On Riddles and Other Enigmatic Modes.* New York: Oxford University Press.

Hast, Dorothea. 1993. "Performance, Transformation, and Community: Contra Dance in New England. *Dance Research Journal* 25: 21–32.

Hufford, David. 1983. "Folk Healers." In *Handbook of American Folklore,* ed. Richard Dorson, 306–13. Bloomington: Indiana University Press, 1983.

Hufford, David J. 1982. *The Terror That Comes in the Night: An Experience-Centered Study of Supernatural Assault Traditions.* Philadelphia: University of Pennsylvania Press.

Hurston, Zora Neale. [1934] 1990. *Jonah's Gourd Vine.* New York: Harper Perennial.

———. [1935] 1990. *Mules and Men.* New York: Harper Perennial.

————. [1937] 1998. *Their Eyes Were Watching God*. New York: Harper Perennial.

————. [1938] 1990. *Tell My Horse*. New York: Harper Perennial.

————. [1939] 1991. *Moses, Man of the Mountain*. New York: Harper Perennial.

————. [1942] 1996. *Dust Tracks on a Road*. New York: Harper Perennial.

————. [1948] 1991. *Seraph on the Suwanee*. New York: Harper Perennial.

Lipman, Doug. 1999. *Improving Your Storytelling: Beyond the Basics for All Who Tell Stories in Work or Play*. Little Rock, AR: August House Publishers, Inc.

Lipsitz, George. 1981. *Class and Culture in Cold War America: "A Rainbow at Midnight."* New York: Praeger.

Long, Lucy. 2004. *Culinary Tourism*. Lexington: University Press of Kentucky.

Lüthi, Max. 1976. *Once upon A Time: On the Nature of Fairy Tales*. Bloomington: Indiana University Press.

Malone, Bill C. 1993. *Singing Cowboys and Musical Mountaineers: Southern Culture and the Roots of Country Music*. Athens: University of Georgia Press.

McNeil, W. K. 1996. "American Folklore Scholarship: The Early Years." In *American Folklore: An Encyclopedia*, ed. Jan Harold Brunvand, 17–23. New York: Garland.

Meyer, Richard E. 1993. *Ethnicity and the American Cemetery*. Bowling Green, Ohio: Bowling Green State University Popular Press.

Meyer, Richard E., ed. 1992. *Cemeteries and Gravemarkers: Voices of American Culture*. Logan: Utah State University.

Mooney, Bill, and David Holt. 1996. *The Storyteller's Guide: Storytellers Share Advice for the Classroom, Boardroom, Showroom, Podium, Pulpit, and Center Stage*. Little Rock, AR: August House.

Narayan, Kirin. 1989. *Storytellers, Saints, and Scoundrels: Folk Narrative in Hindu Religious Teaching*. Philadelphia: University of Pennsylvania Press.

O Súilleabháin, Seán. 1967. *Irish Wake Amusements*. Cork: The Mercier Press.

Pellowski, Anne. 1977. *The World of Storytelling*. New York: R. R. Bowker.

Quigley, Colin. 1994. "A Hearing to Designate the Square Dance the American Folk Dance of the United States: Cultural Politics and an American Vernacular Dance Form." In *Seventeenth Symposium of the Study Group on Ethnochoreology 1992 Proceedings: Dance and its Socio-Political Aspects, Dance and Costume*, ed. Irene Loutzake, 87–88. Nafplion, Greece: Peloponnesian Folklore Foundation.

Roberts, Keith A. 1990. *Religion in Sociological Perspective*. Belmont, CA: Wadsworth.

Rodriguez, Sylvia. 1994. "Defended Boundaries, Precarious Elites: The Arroyo Seco Matachines Dance." *Journal of American Folklore* 107: 248–267.

Santino, Jack. 1998. *The Hallowed Eve: Dimensions of Culture in a Calendar Festival in Northern Ireland*. Lexington: University Press of Kentucky.

Santino, Jack, ed. 2000. *Halloween and Other Festivals of Death and Life*. Knoxville: University of Tennessee Press.

Sobol, Joseph Daniel. 1999. *The Storytellers' Journey: An American Revival*. Urbana : University of Illinois Press.

————. *The House between Earth and Sky: Harvesting New American Folktales.* Portsmouth, NH: Teacher Ideas Press, 2005.

Stone, Kay. 1988. *Burning Brightly: New Light on Old Tales Told Today.* Ontario and Orchard Park, CA: Broadview Press.

Stotter, Ruth. 1996. *About Story: Writings on Stories and Storytelling 1980–1994.* Stinson Beach, CA: Stotter Press,

————. 1998. *The Golden Axe and Other Folk Tales of Compassion and Greed.* Stinson Beach, CA: Stotter Press.

————. 2002. *More about Story: Writings on Stories and Storytelling 1995–2001.* Stinson Beach, CA: Speaking Out Press.

Taylor, Archer. 1985. *The Proverb and an Index to "The Proverb."* New York: Peter Lang.

Toelken, Barre. 1991. "Ethnic Selection and Intensification in the Native American Powwow." In *Creative Ethnicity: Symbols and Strategies of Contemporary Ethnic Life,* ed. Stephen Stern and John Allan Cicala, 137–56. Logan: Utah State University Press.

Toelken, J. Barre. 1969. "The 'Pretty Language' of Yellowman: Genre, Mode, and Texture in Navaho Coyote Narratives." *Genre* 2: 211–35, reprinted as "The 'Pretty Languages' [*sic*] of Yellowman: Genre, Mode, and Texture in Navaho Coyote Narratives," in *Folklore Genres,* ed. Dan Ben-Amos, 146–70. Austin: University of Texas Press, 1976.

Trotter, Robert T., II, and Juan A. Chavira. 1981. *Curanderismo.* Athens: University of Georgia Press.

Turner, Victor, ed. 1982. *Celebration: Studies in Festivity and Ritual.* Washington, D.C.: Smithsonian Institution Press.

Utley, Francis Lee. 1958. *The Study of Folk Literature: Its Scope and Use.* Indiana: The American Folklore Society.

Vlach, John Michael, and Simon J. Bronner, eds. 1992. *Folk Art and Art Worlds.* Logan: Utah State University Press.

Ward, Gerald W. R., Abaigeal Duda, Pamela A. Parmal, Sue Welsh Reed, Gilian Ford Shallcross, and Carol Troyen. 2001. *American Folk: Folk Art from the Collection of the Museum of Fine Arts, Boston.* Boston: Museum of Fine Arts.

Warner, Marina. 1994. *From the Beast to the Blond: On Fairy Tales and Their Tellers.* New York: Farrar, Straus and Giroux.

Zipes, Jack, ed. 2001. *The Great Fairy Tale Tradition: From Straparola and Basile to the Brothers Grimm.* New York: W. W. Norton.

Zumwalt, Rosemary L. 1996. "Franz Boas (1858–1942)." In *American Folklore: An Encyclopedia,* ed. Jan Harold Brunvand, 94–95. New York: Garland.

Five

Contexts

As demonstrated in the last chapter, folklore and story have more shapes, colors, and sizes than a kaleidoscope. As the human imagination has encompassed its world, it has focused, tried to understand, created, and responded to what it experienced. Over time, etiological stories were invented to explain the beginnings of things. Magic emerged so humans could feel some sort of power over events, particularly natural events, that were threatening and mysterious. Stratifications between people evolved based on economic power, geographic location, aesthetic progress, and even the tones of the skin. Religious or belief systems of every imaginable kind were invented and still new ones emerge. Wars were and are fought, lives are lost, boundaries are changed, and ancient societies are disrupted and sometimes destroyed all in the name of one god or another. In the midst of all of this, and more, there is great beauty. Human beings have a need for creating and interpreting, and they also have a need to be entertained and distracted from the sometimes mundane and repetitive acts of eating, sleeping, and working.

And so, folklore and story have been tossed about and interpreted in thousands of ways from morality plays to megaplex cinema to entertain, to teach, and to shape generation after generation. This chapter is a discussion of some of the common venues for folklore and story over time and place. Some folklore, that is, expressive human culture, is beautiful and edifying, and some folklore is disturbing and almost haunting. Again, we will take a colorful trip through time and touch the multifaceted worlds of drama, literature, art, film, music, storytelling festivals, and even television. These are the worlds of performed and created folklore and story.

FOLKLORE AND STORY IN DRAMA

Folk drama, that acting out of stories for entertainment and for teaching, takes place in all cultures. Folk stories told through dramatic presentations may be impromptu and largely unplanned or they may be elaborately rehearsed productions. The narrative, most often performed by human actors, may also be presented by puppets, pantomime, shadow figures, or even figures or pictures displayed on story boards. Long ago, folk dramas began with a ritual belief, and as rites of various kinds in honor of various spirits or gods were performed, both publicly and privately, a meaningful story was played out. The purposes of these rites and rituals, present in all cultures, are long lost to contemporary understanding. When we look at photographs of the early cave paintings in France and Spain, and when elaborate costumes or sculptures of thespians from long ago are found, we wonder what the dramatizations were, and who performed them. Who watched, and how much meaning did the performances have?

In the early days of Greece, possibly around 600 B.C.E., scattered city states *(polis)* dominated the terrain, and Athens ultimately emerged as the Athenian Empire. By 400 B.C.E., theatrical competitions were well established, and Sophocles (496 B.C.E.–406 B.C.E.) Began to compete against the established playwright, Aeschylus (525 B.C.E.–456 B.C.E.).

Though Sophocles wrote over 120 plays, only 7 have survived. However, the themes of those plays have become so famous over the centuries that they continue to have influence in everyday lives today. The stories of Oedipus the King, with theories of male competition and mother worship made famous by the psychologist Sigmund Freud, still linger in the minds of people who read broadly. These ancient plays incorporated the folk dramas of family and everyday conflicts and triumphs, the same dramas played out in today's families.

The Romans patterned much of their culture and behavior after the Greeks. Pantomime, popular in the second century C.E., was accompanied by music and perhaps resembled a ballet (Shelton 1988: 341). The story of Paris's choice, the beautiful Helen, was the cause of the Trojan War, and to reenact the old story, and oral tradition, was a popular pastime. Apuleius, born about 124 C.E., wrote a text called *The Golden Ass.* In it, he described a play about the Trojan prince Paris. It begins:

> There appeared on stage a young man representing the Trojan prince, Paris, gorgeously costumed in a cloak of foreign design which flowed down from his shoulders. On his head was a golden tiara. He pretended to be a shepherd tending his flocks. Next there appeared a radiantly fair young boy, naked except for

The ancient Greek Achilles mourning the death of his good friend Patroklos during the Trojan War.

a small cloak which covered his left shoulder. His long golden hair attracted everyone's eyes. It flowed down his back but did not conceal his beautiful little golden wings. This wings and the herald's staff he held in his hand indicated that he represented Mercury, the messenger god. He danced toward the actor representing Paris and offered him the golden apple which he was holding in his right hand. By his gestures, he informed him of Jupiter's command and then immediately danced gracefully away, out of our sight. (Shelton 1988: 339–40. Quote from Apuleius, *The Golden Ass,* 10.30.32)

This passage describes one kind of carefully planned drama from the ancient world. The folk mythology represented by symbolic costuming, props, and gestures suggests that the mythic themes were well known and carefully woven into this carefully prepared performance. In the India, China, Japan, and other parts of this early world, other folk dramas, equally dramatic, were being performed. In India, the ancient stories of the *Ramayana* were shared and passed along and are still performed with countless departures and variations from the classical Sanskrit text. This long, oral poem is recited frequently, and a televised version of the epic was created, presented, and so well received that it was soon followed by another televised epic, the

Mahabharata. Dramatic narration of the sacred texts is a continuing tradition, and the entire *Ramayana* is sometimes recited in daily segments. Sometimes just a section of it is recited and the teller expounds on the moral points made. That is followed with an interactive discussion with the listeners.

In China, sometimes called the land of the dragons, dramas and performances of myths, legends, stories of ghosts, spirits, and other complex and multilayered narratives have been performed for thousands of years. An ideal of the Chinese stage was that every play should carry a moral message. Like the Greek chorus, a singing actor is present who sometimes repeats the chief events of the play and then expresses his opinion of the moral conduct of the characters. Scenery was of minor consideration in Chinese drama:

> If some character must climb a mountain, pantomimic motions assume the presence of a granite hill. If a criminal is to be executed, it is accomplished with a bamboo pole and traditional movements on the part of the actor. He, the criminal, wails a confession of guilt, walks to one side of the stage and stands under a bamboo pole on which a cloth is tied; he indicates strangulation by throwing back his head and looking up to heaven. If, in a stage story, a general goes upon a journey, the scene is not changed to transport one's mind to another place, instead the soldier cracks a whip, dashes across the stage to a crash of cymbals, and announces that he has arrived. To dismount from his absent steed he pirouettes upon one foot and drops his whip; to mount he turns upon the other foot and picks up his whip. If a plot demands that a fairy enter in a chariot of clouds, a feminine figure advances bearing horizontally two flags upon which clouds and wheels are painted; she is accompanied by another actor in the ubiquitous blue cotton of the Chinese workman. (Buss 1922: n.p.)

The history of the earliest roots of Chinese drama is unclear, but that Chinese theater existed long before the Christian era has been verified. Some historians suggest that Chinese theater was established by an emperor about 700 B.C.E., and that the writers of that century applied themselves to the development of poetic drama. Some of the lore about early Chinese drama reflects the mixed feelings in the culture concerning the art:

> We read of an emperor who lived seventeen hundred years before the Christian era who was commended for having forbidden certain stage conventions; another ruler of a pre-Christian dynasty was deprived of funeral honors because he was thought to have too much enjoyed the theater; and a third emperor was

advised to exclude actors from his court.... During the Yüan dynasty, founded in 1280 [C.E.] by the Mongol warrior Kublai Kahn, drama, as it now exists in China, appears to have slipped into being as quietly as a fall of snow overnight, and as far as most historians are concerned with the subject, is an established fact only from this time. (n.p.)

The folk drama of the Japanese differs greatly from both the Sanskrit traditions of India and the morality plays of China. Performances of the *No* (or *Noh*) dramas keep generation after generation of Japanese viewers conscious of the heroes of their history. These plays are stately and stylized and move at an extremely slow pace. The performance may last an hour based on a text of only two or three hundred lines. Very deliberate movements, accompanied by singing, speech, music (three drums and a flute), dancing, and mime combine into a harmonious presentation with no dominating element. Wooden masks are used by main the character and also the characters of women and old people, but the actors are all males. Developed in the fourteenth century, the No performances are aimed at an educated audience and focus on elevated emotions and deeply introspective meditations.

Another form of folk drama, the *Bunraku* puppet tradition, emerged about a thousand years ago and developed into a popular form of entertainment by the mid-seventeenth century. The puppets were remarkably lifelike, with movable eyes, eyebrows, and jaws. Used primarily for entertainment, this art form became a forerunner of the *Ningyo-shibai* marionettes. Like the No, the Ningyo-shibai, a unique form of puppet theater that developed on the Awaji Island, was used not only for entertainment, but to help maintain codes of purity and to control potentially dangerous spiritual forces. The development of marionettes and puppetry in Japan evolved over a long period of time, and scholars who have studied the history of these traditions are concerned about indifference to this ancient folk are among many academics ("Asian Drama" 2003: n.p.).

The popular Japanese *Kabuki* folk drama, which also emerged in the sixteenth and seventeenth centuries, places more emphasis on excitement and conflict. There are more characters, though like the No, the Kabuki uses only male actors. "The most popular play in the Kabuki repertoire is a revenge play entitled *The Treasury of Loyal Retainers.* One interesting facet of Kabuki, perhaps reflecting its popular origins, the Kabuki stage is marked by a walkway *(hanamichi)*, which extends from the stage into the audience and to the back of the auditorium" ("Asian Drama" 2003: n.p.). The Kabuki, in both classical and contemporary style, remains popular in Japan. The deliberate

No performances are less well liked, and performances are restricted to very few theatrical groups. Very few Japanese are interested in them.

Folk dramas are often presented for religious purposes throughout the world. Medieval mystery, miracle, and passion plays often presented traditional religious morality or dogma. One survivor (among many) of these ancient folk plays performed regularly for the citizens continues in the Bavarian region of Germany. The Oberammergau Passion Play has been performed, for the most part, once a decade since the 1600s. An editor's note stated:

> In 1633, the residents of the small Bavarian village of Oberammergau made a vow that, if they were spared from a plague that was sweeping the countryside, they would perform a Passion Play in perpetuity. Legend has it that no more villagers died; and the town has famously kept its vow. Every decade for centuries, the people of Oberammergau have presented their play. As described by theatrical historian James Shapiro, Oberammergau is a fascinating cultural, commercial, and religious saga. ("Passion of the Crisis" 2005: 1)

This event involves about half of the town's 5,200 men, women, and children, and "Eligibility is limited to those born in Oberammergau, those who have lived there twenty years or those who married villagers (which cuts this probationary period in half" (2). The town identifies itself with this event, and a folk culture has grown up around it. Homes are painted with biblical scenes, streets are named for biblical items and events, and the Stations of the Cross were created as an official exhibit in 2000. Over hundreds of years' practice, the little German town has become a backdrop and context for the play.

In Ireland, the folk custom of mumming at the Christmas season was well known and practiced for many centuries. Actors would arrived unannounced at various houses and enact a combat drama. Often St. George (or some other well-known hero figure) would fight with the Turkish Knight (or another non-Christian figure), and the actor playing the doctor would aid the knight, who in turn would pledge allegiance and loyalty to the hero. These folk plays are not commonly performed anymore. Attempts at revival have largely failed, and other activities have taken the place of mumming. The practice represented the old ways of rural Ireland, and memories of it were carried to America by Irish immigrants.

No one quite knows the history of mumming, but some scholars suggest that it may have emerged from rituals to insure agricultural success. Types of mumming, that is, combat dramas, have been recorded in many places of the world, but the underlying function of the ritual drama has differed with different cultures. Henry Glassie, folklorist, suggested that in Ireland the purpose was entertainment and encouragement of community feelings. On the origin, Glassie suggested that "Mumming does have a long history, running back to the seventeenth century and possibly beyond to a misty pre-Christian dawn. There is a description of mumming from the city of Cork, in 1685" (Glassie 1975: 57, 58). The custom may have been carried to Ulster in the seventeenth century but ceased for the most part between the Easter Uprising of 1916 and the Civil War of 1922 (135) Now and then, groups assemble, practice, and perform the mummer's art in parts of Ireland, Newfoundland, and even the West Indies, "but such productions were rare, except as performed by professional and semiprofessional actors in the context of folk revival" (Taft 1996: 208).

In the early days of the Southwest United States and Mexico, Spanish priests brought the Christian religion to the people, and out of that tradition developed the *pastorelas*. These are both publically and privately performed plays that tell of Mary and Joseph's search for lodgings in Bethlehem and the birth of Christ. They are enacted every evening between December 16 and December 24. The plays vary, and some pastorelas may act out conflicts between Lucifer and St. Michael over the spirit of the baby Christ. Laughter and enjoyment accompany the more serious parts of the presentations because the shepherds and other peasants provide comic relief by being presented in humorous situations. These plays delight and instruct viewers of all ages.

Another folk drama performed at the time of the pastorelas are the *Posadas*. In this tradition, people go to a home and sing folk songs while standing outside. Lighted candles are held, and the songs again tell the story surrounding the birth of Christ. In the most traditional Posada celebration, there may be a boy and girl dressed like Mary and Joseph. Many verses are sung while the singers beg to be admitted into the house. Once inside, a Christmas party, complete with the fruit- and candy-filled piñata takes place. The stick used to break the piñata represents the faith of Christ put to good use by the children who use it. The folk tradition is that they break the beautiful piñata and release the prizes for the use of all people, just as Christ came to teach love for all people (Dumois 2005: 1,2).

In the United States, a Christmas pageant is often enacted in churches and sometimes in schools across ethnic, regional, and religious boundaries. Sometimes the story of Christ's birth is told, and sometimes the focus is on Santa Claus, but skits and music on a wide number of themes are performed and shared, and a sense of goodwill and community is shared. At other times of the year, American children perform folk dramatizations of stories at summer camps, resorts, and at organized scouting activities. There are many other folk dramas performed in the United States, and the essence of the performance tells a story in a little different way with each presentation.

FOLKLORE AND STORY IN LITERATURE

The use of folklore in the narrative traditions of the world, both oral and literary, is constant and recurrent. Many great works of literary art have been based on oral lore. The ancient writers in Greece and Rome, and the even more ancient bards and tellers in India, China, and Japan, borrowed stories passed to them and told them in their own way. Many of the tales were written, and those narrative carried threads of lore from the past on into our contemporary times. Even the scriptures, including the Hebrew Bible and the Qur'an were first received as oral literature laced with stories and verses passed along from antiquity.

Shakespeare, well known for developing themes he knew into the great plays he wrote, borrowed the theme for *The Taming of the Shrew* from *The Devil's Bet, Romeo and Juliet* from *The Hill of Roses, The Merchant of Venice* from *A Bargain Is a Bargain, Hamlet* from *Ashboy, King Lear* from *Cap-o-Rushes,* and *The Winter's Tale* from *The Flower Princess* (Ryan 2001: 4). Samuel Clemens borrowed themes and dialects for *Tom Sawyer* and *The Adventures of Huckleberry Finn* from the memories of his childhood near the Mississippi River in Missouri. His stories of the early West came directly from his experiences there, and in his texts he repeated stories and anecdotes (folklore) that he had heard while traveling. It is likely that he embellished the lore, as Shakespeare did, but it is folklore after all. The internationally popular Harry Potter books by J. K. Rowling contain a myriad of traditional symbols. From labyrinthine castles and schools to wands, owls, pointed hats, and capes of invisibility, Rowling has infused her story with mythic traditions and folklore to enrich and entertain the readers.

Beloved writers of the twentieth century, from Zora Neale Hurston, John Steinbeck, and Ernest Hemingway to James Thurber and William Faulkner, have used the lore of the people in their stories. Hurston's novels included folkloric items that ranged from Southern porch culture to voodoo; Steinbeck lived with the suffering people he wrote about. He knew their pain and tragedies, and he knew their words. Hemingway traveled the world to gather words and stories and attitudes. He experienced World War II himself and listened to injured troops. Thurber was an observer, and he had the talent to strip expressive culture to a few lines and words. William Faulkner created a mythic or fictional world, populated by generations, based on cultural attitudes and expressions of those attitudes.

In contemporary young adult fiction, a popular and important genre, texts since S. E. Hinton's *The Outsiders* (1967) have attempted to present the real and often raw life of the teen world. Expressed behaviors and human responses, from slang to poetry to nursery rhymes, helps explain themes from school candy sales to proms, unwed pregnancies, drug abuse, and prejudice, vampires, and other popular mythic themes. The writers use familiar, and sometimes not so familiar, folkloric motifs and traditions to present their stories.

From "politically correct" tellings of traditional tales to fractured versions and parodies like Thurber's "The Girl and the Wolf," literary creators have drawn from the world's legacy of lore to enrich their stories. Literature can be manipulated and expressed by talented writers who creatively invent their own worlds. That those worlds of realistic fiction are furnished with items from the oral, material, and customary folklore and belief systems of the world we live in, or that those same elements are used to furnish the fantastic, imaginary worlds they create, is one of the marvels of the creator.

FOLKLORE AND STORY IN ART

For thousands of years, human beings kept their stories alive through memorization and through the use of visual representations. Archeologists and other explorers have found surviving markings, cave paintings, small and mysterious female effigies, relief sculptures, statues, fragments of ornate metalwork, and countless other artifacts that seem to try to speak their stories from the dust of the earth. Intricate gold jewelry with symbolism lost to our present knowledge was found in the ruins of Troy; jade artifacts and statuary was found in the ancient tombs of China, often arranged in very particular ways; remains of Viking ships have been found in Great Britain laden with exquisite jewelry and arms often marked with runes; and from these objects, and thousands more, we have learned that humankind has created objects of art to carry their stories from the earliest time.

The story clothes of the Hmong people are colorful expressions of village life and behaviors. These are intricately embroidered on a blue background and have brightly colored scenes of people and animals. There is no end to the variety of these cloths, and each one carries its own story. The totem poles of the Northwest Haida Indians carry their own stories. Each one represents a different facet of the folklife of the clan, and each represents protection and power. The raven, a trickster figure, appears on many of the totems, and stories of the raven, who furnished the sun, the moon, and the stars for the Haida clan, are numerous and entertaining.

Baskets, rugs, and pottery are probably the most ubiquitous folk art items in the world, and different cultures attach myriad meanings and stories to them. The pine needle baskets of the Oregon coast carry tales of folk wisdom about folk cures and taboos. The intricately woven Navajo baskets tell both traditional and contemporary tales about the people and their history. The handwoven rugs of the Navajo each represent a different tale, and in the Middle East, where the intricate Turkish and Persian rugs are created, an oral direction-giver chants the method for the rug, weaving in anecdotes and tales, as the rug is being created.

The art of folk pottery and the stories attached are also international and constant. One of the reasons we know what we know about the ancient Greek and Roman cultures is the result of pottery decorated with elaborate designs, and more importantly, figures. In those ancient days, the craft of pottery was not held in high esteem. In fact, potters were very poor. It was a necessary craft, countless pots were needed for culinary use, and the buyers were much more interested in what was in the jars than in the jars themselves. To pass the time, and possibly earn a little more from their art, the potters began to compete with glazes and representations on their wares. Images of the Trojan War, of goddesses and gods, and of mythic legends were painted on the pottery and seldom signed. These vases, of varying sizes and complexity, are now worth millions of dollars—apiece!

American folk art ranges broadly in style and use. One of the most interesting types of folk art and story practiced since Colonial days is the art of the American quilt making. The evocative names of quilt patterns: "Wild Goose Chase," "Wedding Ring," "Double Wedding Ring," "Star of Bethlehem," "Tree of Life," "Friendship Ring," and others tell a story in themselves. The quilts were often made by groups of women, and if the quilts could talk, they would tell many stories. The designs were passed along from person to person, often by word of mouth or by simple drawn patterns.

One of the most interesting quilts from the 1800s was made by an African American woman named Harriet Powers. Harriet was born a slave in Athens, Georgia, around 1837. She could neither read nor write, but she created many quilts of her own, artful design. One, a quilt of ten squares, depicted "stories of Adam and Eve, Noah, Job, Jonah, Moses, and Christ. Other [quilts] celebrated natural events such as a meteor shower and an extreme cold snap when 'isicles [*sic*] formed from the breath of a mule' and a man was frozen at his jug of liquor. The square in the center of the bottom row features Betts, 'the independent hog which ran 500 miles from Ga. To Va.'" (Ward, 2001: 93). Powers was paid very little for her work, and no one knows how she learned her stories, but that she did is evident in the imagery of her quilts.

FOLKLORE AND STORY IN FILM

It is probable that the most well known films to be based on folkloric traditions are the Walt Disney animated fairy tales of *Snow White and the Seven Dwarves* (1937), *Cinderella* (1950), and *Beauty and the Beast* (1991). Many films about vampires, werewolves, urban lore, and horror have been created and received well by moviegoers and VCR/DVD users. Books are commonly adapted by screenwriters, and stories such as *The Never Ending Story* (1984), *The Princess Bride* (1987), and *Friday the Thirteenth* (1980) have remained very popular.

Cult films, meaning that a fan group has created itself and the films are run and rerun, have developed around many films. *The Princess Bride* is one, and *Monty Python and the Holy Grail* (1975) is another. The Monty Python film is a parody of the Arthurian cycle of tales, and it depicts King Arthur framed by a contemporary murder investigation. The mythical king and his knights face untold horrors such as the Black Knight, who is hacked but somehow survives, the perilous Castle Anthrax, a killer rabbit, and other peculiar threats. Another cult film that represents teen life and the everyday folklife of a rural, Idaho town is *Napoleon Dynamite* (2004). In this story, Napoleon suffers the anxiety of being a less-than-top-of-the-heap teenager, but he is bright and kind and happily survives his adventures.

Documentaries about various ethnic groups and nationalities and adapted books, both nonfiction and fiction, rewritten by screenwriters, have used many strategies to best represent the stories being told.

> In *The Poetics,* Aristotle distinguished between two types of fictional narratives: *Mimesis* (showing) and *diegesis* (telling). *Mimesis* is the province of the live theater, where the events "tell themselves." *Diegesis,* the province of the literary epic and the novel, is a story told by a narrator who is sometimes reliable, sometimes not. Cinema combines both forms of storytelling and hence is a more complex medium, with a wider range of narrative techniques at its disposal. (Giannetti 2002: 334)

We can see in various contemporary films how these two strategies are implemented. In the *Star Wars* films, both showing and telling increase the drama of the scenes. The *Star Wars* films are built on a framework of mythology and the adventures of the hero. Joseph Campbell, a mythologist, was an advisor for the first film, and symbolism is used throughout all of the *Star Wars* series. For instance, "The monster masks that are put on people in Star Wars represent the real monster-force in the modern world. When the mask of Darth Vader is removed, you see an unformed man, one who has not developed as a human individual. He's a bureaucrat, living not in terms of himself, but in terms of an imposed system" (Flowers 1988: 145).

From *E.T.: The Extra-Terrestrial* (1982) to *Forrest Gump* (1994), we see filmmakers interpreting narratives on a symbolic level. The universal human condition of innocence in childhood, the maturation process, simple pleasures, ambition, fear, failure, and triumph are elements that are used in films to encourage us to buy the tickets and support the industry. Expressive culture, presented with unique insights and twists, helps us to understand our own life journeys a little better.

FOLKLORE AND STORY IN MUSIC

Folk music of many nationalities in the United States can be heard at ethnic festivals and other public events. Many lyrics are traditional and carry stories of the culture's tradition. Often church groups have dinners and music to raise funds for their private schools, and the home-cooked food and enthusiasm of the traditional musicians and singers is a rich experience for everyone. The Greek tradition in the United States includes lively music. Combinations of string, wind, and percussion instruments accompany both circle and line dancing. The dancers hold hands and move through various steps, and onlookers are invited to join in. Sometimes an instrument called a *santoúri,* a trapezoid-shaped dulcimer played with two covered wooden mallets, is played. Recently, another unusual Greek instrument, the *bouzoúki,* a long-necked, mandolin-like stringed instrument, has become used more frequently. Stories embedded in the words and sounds of the music, mournful and slow, romantic and light, or quick and fiery, represent the moods and temper of the Greeks. A culturally proud and traditional people, the music reflects their many moods.

The folk music of the Appalachian region of the United States was a part of the urban folk music revival of the 1940s and 1950s, and it was also reflected in the counterculture of young Americans in the 1960s. The lyrics told stories, and singers like Joan Baez and Bob Dylan remain a strong part of today's popular culture. Country music, with its ties to the rural past, has remained popular in many regions in the United States. Its popularity is increasing in cities in part because the country lyrics tell a story. The music seems to reflect middle-American, blue-collar values, and suggests that the idealized past had to be better than the present.

African American music has been intriguing to folklorists and ethnomusicologists since the nineteenth century. Field and work songs, the spirituals that could be slow and sad or lively and hopeful, the rap music of the 1920s and 1930s, and blues and jazz that wound their way up to St. Louis, Chicago, and other northern cities, have entertained and comforted all Americans. The love ballads, the story songs, the hymns, and other folk lyrics share the black traditions. The narratives the songs share contain the African American culture and history, and the music has always been an integral part of their cultural expression.

The prairies of southwest Louisiana are the home of the Cajun people. These are descendants of Acadians who settled in Louisiana between 1764 and 1803 after being deported by the British from Nova Scotia. Their distinctive language is a mixture of French, English, and the influence of other languages. Their music has enjoyed a revival since the 1960s and 1970s, and again their songs contain traditional chants and texts. Cajun songs and storytelling include animal tales, magic stories, jokes, lies, and tall tales, and the fun-loving Cajun people enjoy participation in the annual Mardi Gras celebration held just before the fast days of Lent. They appear in parades and fetes, telling stories, playing traditional tricks, and sharing their lively, unique music.

Ethnomusicology is an interdisciplinary study that involves work in psychology, sociology, linguistics, art, dance, and literary criticism. The following paragraph explains the important work of the ethnomusicologists in relation to the study of folklore and story in music.

> Work in ethnomusicology since 1970 has focused on two kinds of problems affecting musical traditions in the past and the present: (1) musical thought and behavior in specific and often remote, small-scale cultures; and (2) music whose nature has been affected by change of context, tourism, or ideology or by other factors such as the mass media and the cassette industry [and the CD industry]. The first kind of study is guided principally by the methods of cultural anthropology or folklore; the second, more by sociological analysis and cross-cultural explanation in aesthetics or semiotics [words and language]. A third kind of problem involves music learning and perception and is based in the methods of cognitive anthropology or cognitive [how people learn or know] psychology. All of these approaches have been informed at a deeper level by developments in critical theory (sociology) [study of groups], cultural praxis (anthropology) [practice], and hermeneutics (philosophy). (Porter 1996: 231–32)

Folklorist and others are examining the cultural dynamics of music and the developments ethnic and folk music traditions are undergoing in this changing world. Many traditional cultures are endangered because of encroachment from other groups, and the hope is that the traditions will be protected and continued for generations to come.

FOLKLORE AND STORY IN TELEVISION

Folklore and mythology, jokes, anecdotes, proverbs, fables, and other forms of oral folklore are used in television presentations hundreds of times each day. American television is a part of the culture. It contributes to it, and it draws from it to interest the viewers. From Saturday morning cartoons that draw their themes from heroic tales and narratives to commercials that fill the time between breaks in sports televising and just about everything else telecast, folklore is alive and active on our television screens.

Linda Dégh, folklorist and author of *American Folklore and the Mass Media* (1994), quoted a study that reveals the profuse presence of folklore items in everyday television:

> In one study of folklore as presented on television, Tom Burns, with *TV Guide* in hand, sat in front of the screen from early morning until late at night on 15 May 1969 (Burns 1969). He watched programs chosen from the four main networks and a local station in order to compile a representative sample of folklore on American television. During his nineteen-hour vigil, Burns did not pay special attention to any particular genre (such as the folktale) or to one kind of TV show (such as commercials), but indiscriminately recorded every bit of folkloric material. He reported a total of 101 "traditional items and themes" which he qualified as "true" folklore. This count indicates that in every hour of TV broadcasting, an average of at least five "traditional" folklore items appeared. (Dégh 1994: 37)

Folklore, as Dégh suggests, is a dynamic historical process, and it adapts to the cultural needs of each period. One of the assignments I give my Myth, Legend, and Folktale classes is to identify the use of those three genres in advertisements or commercials on television. Responses over the years have been in the hundreds, and they have ranged over various sources from the Nordic Vikings to Greek heroes to Indian gurus. Angels, devils, talking animals, and dancing cupids are only a few of the advertising ploys they have seen. The Burns study quoted above was collected several years ago, but I don't think there would be much difference in the result if it were conducted today. Folklore and story are the elements on which we build our cultures, and it is true that they are used over and over again, according to the time and place, to shape traditions and to sell products.

FOLKLORE AND STORY IN STORYTELLING FESTIVALS

The revival in storytelling, that is, the recitation of a prose or poetic narrative by a single teller, and of storytelling festivals in particularly the United States and Canada, has been enormous. Hundreds of local groups and centers have sprung up, and not only do many libraries offer storytelling hours for the children, but university drama departments are offering regular credit courses in storytelling training. There are issues in the storytelling arena, such as the modern recontextualization of old tales to adapt the way women are represented in many traditional narrative accounts; thus, there is much academic discussion about the direction of the popular storytelling movement. There are many organized storytelling communities, individual tellers, conferences, festivals, and tales, and the American Folklore Society has a opened a section for storytellers in addition to a section of folk narrative.

As stated earlier in this text, storytelling by teachers and librarians began in the late nineteenth and early twentieth centuries in order to encourage children to read books. The tradition has continued well through the twentieth century and has escalated in the twenty-first. Storytelling has become not only a didactic and/or entertaining activity for children, but it has become an active part of adult life in America. From stand-up comics telling tales on television and in clubs to international storytelling conventions, conferences, and festivals, storytelling has become a recognized part of the American way of life.

Story has also been recognized as an important part of formal, academic language arts training. The interactive style of many contemporary storytellers has use in the academic classroom, where an exchange of information is a better way of learning than the traditional, talking-head lecture format. From Sunday school, to vacation Bible school, to summer camp, to festivals throughout the world, storytelling is finally receiving the recognition and status that it once held in the ancient world. Why? Because people need to feel human connection. We live in a technological world, and the warmth of a human storyteller, and the warmth of interaction with a human storyteller, is a need that many people of all ages seem to have.

In Joseph Sobol's *The Storyteller's Journey*, we are informed that the storytelling revival is a part of a larger process of cultural revitalization. The preeminent revival organization, the National Association for the Preservation and Perpetuation of Storytelling (NAPPS), in Jonesborough, Tennessee, founded by Jimmy Neil Smith in 1973, has blossomed into a national and international network of arts professionals. Sobol explains some of the underpinnings of that first national storytelling festival:

Politically, the contemporary storytelling movement grew out of the sixties' cultural radicalism and the seventies' inward-turning politics of personal growth. It can certainly be viewed as a sublimation of politics in the realm of performance, a retreat to a constructed communal dream world in which intractable issues that were rending American society—such issues as war and peace, ecological destruction, and racial and ethnic strife—could be faced and overcome in an imaginative transport, bypassing the physical realm of bullets and blood, in the hope of advancing the healing process to a point where more gruesome plot turns could be avoided. (Sobol 1999: 15)

Family stories, conversational anecdotes, performance tales, history telling, and even songs and poems can carry significant impact on both tellers and listeners. It is through sharing the myriad stories that the culture of understanding is transmitted from one person to another. Marni Gillard, a professional storyteller and former teacher and professor, reminds us that stories can come from any source, and she encourages teachers to "allow the children to *tell* their stories . . . " (Gillard 1996: xiii). Another storyteller and folklorist, Ruth Stotter, reminds us that "A newer trend is the telling of traditional oral narratives, especially by psychotherapists, to help people obtain insight and heal psychological wounds. Therapeutic storytelling has been popularized by storyteller authors like Joseph Campbell, Robert Bly, and Jack Zipes" (Stotter 2002: 3). Verena Kast also wrote a text about *Folktales as Therapy* (1995), which contains six tales and their easy-to-follow interpretations.

We know that storytellers cannot quite compete with television, films, and the Internet, but we also know that things that last have meaning in society. The revival of these ancient forms, whether traditional or nontraditional, public or private, told in school or outside it, has something important to say about human connection and need. We live in an age of rapid and irreversible change, and technology has connected the world as never before. Perhaps it is through story that we will remember the deep responsibilities we all have within the human family.

WORKS CITED

"Asian Drama, Asian Literature." 2003. AllRefer.com. Available at: http://reference. allrefer.com/encyclopedia/A/Asiandra-japanese-drama.html. Accessed 14 October 2005.

Burns, Tom. 1969. "Folklore in the Mass Media." *Folklore Forum* 2: 90–106.

Buss, Kate. 1922. "Origin of the Chinese Drama." In *Studies in the Chinese Drama.* New York: , ed. Jonathan Cape and Harrison Smith. Available at: http://www. theatrehistory.com/asian/chinese001.html. Accessed 13 October 2005.

Dégh, Linda. 1994. *American Folklore and the Mass Media*. Bloomington: Indiana University Press.

Dumois, Luis. 2005. "Inside Mexico—The Series: *Posadas, Pastorelas, and Nacimientos.*" Available at: http://www.mexconnect.com/mex_travel/ldumois/ldcposadas.html. Accessed 14 October 2005.

Flowers, Betty Sue, ed. 1988. *The Power of Myth/Joseph Campbell*. New York/ London: Doubleday.

Giannetti, Louis. 2002. *Understanding Movies.*9th ed. Upper Saddle River, NJ: Prentice Hall.

Gillard, Marni. 1996. *Storyteller, Story Teacher: Discovering the Power of Storytelling for Teaching and Living*. Portland, ME: Stenhouse Publishers.

Glassie, Henry. 1975. *All Silver and No Brass: An Irish Christmas Mumming*. Philadelphia: University of Pennsylvania Press.

Hinton, S. E. 1967. *The Outsiders*. New York: Dell.

"The Passion of the Crisis." 2005. *Jewsweek Magazine*. Available at: http://www. jewsweek.com/bin/en.jsp?enPage = BlankPage&enDisplay = view&enDisp What = object&enDispWho=Article^I1065&enZone=Articles&enVersion=O&. Accessed 14 October 2005.

Kast, Verena. 1995. *Folktales as Therapy*. New York: Fromm International Publishing.

Porter, James. 1996. "Ethnomusicology." In *American Folklore: An Encyclopedia*, ed. Jan Harold Brunvand, 230–38. New York: Garland.

Ryan, Patrick. 2001. *Shakespeare's Storybook: Folk Tales That Inspired the Bard*. Cambridge, ME: Barefoot Books.

Shelton, Jo-Ann. 1988. *As the Romans Did: A Source Book in Roman Social History*. New York: Oxford University Press.

Sobol, Joseph Daniel. 1999. *The Storyteller's Journey: An American Revival*. Urbana: University of Illinois Press.

Stotter, Ruth. 2002. *More about Story: Writings on Stories and Storytelling 1995–2001*. Stinson Beach, CA: Speaking Out Press

Taft, Michael. 1996. "Folk Drama." In *American Folklore: An Encyclopedia*, ed. Jan Harold Brunvand, 208–10. New York: Garland.

Ward, Gerald W. R., Abaigeal Duda, Pamela A. Parmal, Sue Welsh Reed, Gilian Ford Shallcross, and Carol Troyen. 2001. *American Folk: Folk Art from the Collection of the Museum of Fine Arts, Boston*. Boston: Museum of Fine Arts.

Glossary

Aarne-Thompson. Antti Aarne (1867–1925) collected and created the first tale-type index, which was called *Verzeichnis der Märchentypen* (Index of Folktale Types). It identified and classified animal tales, ordinary folktales, and humorous tales. Later, Stith Thompson (1885–1976) twice revised and expanded Aarne's type index and added formula tales and unclassified tales, which made five generic subsets. Available to folklorists now are Aarne-Thompson indexes, which classify folktales from specific countries around the world.

Acculturation. Cultural changes that occur as a result of contact between societies. The contact may be brief or extended. This also occurs when an individual adapts to a culture that is not the one into which he or she was born.

Aesthetics. The theory of beauty and the perceived or psychological response to beauty as interpreted by individual cultures. Contemporary use of the concept applies it to all types of art. The ancient Greeks used the concept of aesthetics in reference only to material things.

Aetiological Legend. An origin tale. *See also* Etiologic Tale.

Allegory. An allegory is a story that has symbolic or hidden meaning that lies outside of the narrative. The characters, objects, and action in the story are used to teach ideas, moral principles, or other ideas. Many folk and fairy tales have symbolic meaning; for instance, "Rapunzel" is often interpreted as a story about maturation and dangers of the adult world; "Hansel and Gretel" is an allegory about good overcoming evil and the independence, cunning, and practical resourcefulness of children; "Sleeping Beauty" is a tale representing death and resurrection.

Alliteration. Repetition of the initial consonant sound. An example of alliteration in a typical and familiar nursery rhyme would be: Peter Piper picked a peck of pickled peppers. If Peter Piper picked a peck of pickled peppers, how many pickled peppers did Peter Piper pick?

Anecdote. In folklore, a short, entertaining, verbal account of an event that really happened. It may be autobiographical, biographical, or historical.

Animal Tale. A short, simple folktale in which animals are the major characters. Trickster tales often feature animals.

Animism. The belief that animals, plants, and other physical matter, such as minerals and water, have souls.

Anthropology. Past and present study of human beings and their varied cultures. A social science, the focus of anthropological study varies. Some of the branches of anthropology are: cultural anthropology (study of invented cultural behaviors), physical anthropology (the study of physical characteristics of humans), archeology (study of past life by site excavation), aesthetic anthropology (the study of human perception of beauty).

Anthropomorphic. A practice of giving gods, animals, or inanimate things human shape or characteristics. Stories with talking animals or trees are anthropomorphic. The most common use of the anthropomorphic concept is in religion or belief systems, in which gods are often described as having human strengths and weaknesses. Many stories continue to be told of Zeus, the chief Greek god, who was said to have the human weakness of chasing after unwilling but beautiful women. Hermes, the Greek trickster, continues to be presented as a deceitful character ready to serve his own interests.

Antiphonal. Singing, chanting, or creating poetry in a style in which both sides are verbally performing. There is dynamic, verbal call-and-response interaction between the two sides such as in some religious services in which the congregation responds with a line of scripture to the minister's line of scripture or song.

Archetype. Carl Jung (1875–1961) was a European psychologist who theorized that human beings share a collective knowledge called the collective unconscious. Archetypes are images, symbols, and motifs that seem to have universal meaning and shared understanding among the human family because of this shared "collective unconscious." Motifs and imagery in folk and fairy tales are thought to make logical sense to people across the world because of shared and recognizable *archetypal* elements such as wands, which seem to wield power, or birds, which often represent freedom. *See also* Collective Unconscious.

Archive. A repository in which collections of fieldwork, public and private records, artifacts, and documents are stored. The collected folklore is arranged by types, informants, regions, and collectors. The collections can be retrieved and examined under controlled circumstances in order to protect the materials.

Artifact. A material object made by humans that represents the style and tradition of a culture. Common artifacts are pottery, baskets, and rugs, but there are countless other examples of artifacts from around the world.

Artistic Communication. Verbal folklore traditional and often familiar communication in small groups. It may be communication in the form of anecdotes, stories, jokes, proverbs, gossip, or many other forms of narrative exchange. It is artistic because it carries cultural meaning, and its influence in bonding participants helps them to understand and maintain their cultural milieu.

Ballad. Usually of unknown origin, a ballad is a poetic song, romantic or sentimental, that tells a story in short stanzas and repetitive, rhythmic form. The story of the ballad is often folkloric, having been transmitted from person to person, and both oral tellers and singers often use this form in their performances.

Bard. An ancient storyteller or singer of epic poems who usually accompanied himself (or herself) on a harp or lyre. This term is commonly used to describe a Celtic minstrel or poet.

Belief. Things people believe. There are concepts and well-defined systems of convictions and assumptions that construct cultures and individual lives. From folk medicine to superstitions, from folk religions to mainstream religions, belief can be a strong and persuasive influence on choice and behavior.

Cante Fable. A folk narrative that includes a song within it to convey the point of the story.

Catch Joke. A catch joke has an unexpected twist at the end that surprises or even embarrasses the listener.

Catch Riddle. Like the catch joke, the catch riddle has an unexpected twist at the end that surprises or even embarrasses the listener.

Clan. A group of people who claim common descent from one ancestor.

Climax. The decisive turning point in a story or drama.

Code-Switching. Individuals who are fluent in more than one language may mix or switch languages in the course of a conversation or even within a sentence. I have observed this practice among people who want to keep parts of their conversation private when they have a sense of being overheard.

Collective Unconscious. Carl Gustav Jung felt that the unconscious part of the mind contained not only the feelings of the individual, but also the results of the collective experience of mankind. *See also* Archetype.

Complex Tales. Complicated narratives with many parts or episodes that build upon one another.

Contagious Magic. Magic that uses clothing or something from the body itself. There is belief that because of the natural connection, that item has power concerning the person to be affected. A person's fingernail clipping, hair, shoe, ring, or other similar items may be used in a ritual cursing or blessing.

Context. In folklore, context refers to the social and physical surroundings in which an item of folklore is used, presented, or collected.

Craftsperson. One who has learned a trade or profession through observation, an apprentice system, or through oral transmission. The most common crafts in the world are pottery, rugs, and baskets; however, "craft" can also refer to oral lore or telling. The Griots, in West Africa, tradition bearers in families, learn the craft of "telling" by oral transmission and observation of members of their kinship clan.

Custom. A social behavior passed on by tradition and enforced by social disapproval of violation of the custom. For instance, in Western culture, it is expected to say please and thank you when requesting a service. To fail to utter these simple words carries a message of ingratitude or even impudence.

Customary Folklore. Things people do. Simple examples of customary folklore would be calendar events such as celebrations of Thanksgiving and the Fourth of July. Further, folk dances, family celebrations (birthdays and anniversaries), religious rituals (such as baby blessings and communion), and even etiquette (writing thank you notes, greeting people) are customary folkloric behaviors.

Diachronic. Occurring at differing times. A study of how cultures may develop and change over time. *See also* Synchronic.

Dialect. Local or regional varieties of speech. For instance, in the American South, it is common to hear and say "Y'all" rather than "All of you." In the intermountain West, it is common to hear "pitcher" when speaking of a "picture." In the Northeast, it is common to hear the "r" sound dropped; one might hear "Havad," rather than "Harvard."

Didactic. Something that is used for the purposes of teaching.

Digital Storytelling. An Internet phenomenon where individuals or groups can post stories and pictures, often biographical, on a public Web site. This method is being used by schools, businesses, and individuals.

Documentation. Folklorists collect information about people, places, and things. The information may be oral or visual, and the method ranges from simple note taking, to recordings, to photographs and videos.

Emic/Etic. In folklore and anthropology, an emic study is performed by a member of the culture, an insider. An etic study is performed by an outside observer.

Enculturation. The natural process humans go through in learning and adapting to the culture in which they are born.

Endless Story. A narrative or story that adds one episode after another (after another and another), and circles around on itself.

Epic. A long, usually dignified narrative about the exploits of a traditional hero. It is an ancient folkloric form, and sometimes the telling of the stories within the epic would continue for days and even weeks.

Etiologic Tale. A narrative that explains the origin of natural phenomena. Stories about how the fox got its tail, or how the fish learned to breathe under water are aetiological tales.

Ethnic Group. A group of people who share a cultural heritage and define themselves as sharing basic social traits.

Ethnomusicology. An interdisciplinary holistic study of the world's music that looks at meaning, style, performance, and context. It is not limited to the study of the music of third world countries, but rather is an all-inclusive study.

Etiologic Tale. An origin tale.

Fable. Using animal characters, the fable is a short narrative that usually conveys a moral at its conclusion.

Fakelore. Richard Dorson suggested in 1950 that literary artists and journalists who make up cultural stories and behaviors are creating fakelore. Genuine folklore emerges from lived culture. Many contemporary folklorists suggest that both fakelore and folklore reflect traditional culture.

Fairy Tale. Usually a narrative or Märchen that has appeared in printed form. *See also* Märchen.

Fan Fiction. A phenomenon of the Internet, fan fiction (or FanFic) is found at countless literary sites where individuals can create their own characters, chapters, and endings to existing fictional works, movies, and television shows. The entered topics range from classical novels to recently published works including fantasy and science fiction.

Festival. A recurring cultural performance of public display. From the Mardi Gras in New Orleans to the county fairs held throughout the United States, festivals reflect community participation.

Fieldwork. A process of gathering information from various places in order to preserve it.

Fish Tale. An exaggerated narrative. A neighbor boy told me that he dropped a four-pronged hook into the water with a bit of bait stuck to each point. In a matter of minutes, he said, he had caught four fish. (Look for a variety of implausibilities in this simple fish tale.)

Folk Art. Usually nonacademic art that usually reflects the practices and attitudes of tightly knit groups of people who share a common background or nationality. The methods are often passed from person to person by vernacular (oral) transmission.

Folk Drama. Often community events that occur on a regular basis. From medieval times, religious rites and plays were performed for onlookers throughout Europe. Today many ancient European towns continue to perform dramas and have drawn onlookers from all over the world.

Folk Narrative. Traditionally, a folk narrative is a story, vernacularly transmitted, that has passed through at least two people. The narrative differs in the telling, and it may be fact or fiction.

Folklore. Traditional forms of expressive culture including vernacular or oral traditions, material and customary traditions, and belief systems.

Folkloristics. Folkloristics can be defined as the collection, classification, analysis, and discussion (oral or written) of traditionally shared expressive forms and behaviors.

Folktale. A folktale is a fictional story, vernacularly transmitted, that is usually used to entertain, though it may be used to teach. The characters may be human or animal, and the time frame and place vary.

Formula Tale. A prose narrative that is more about structure than content. "The House That Jack Built" is an example of a formula tale.

Fractured Fairy Tale. A fairy tale that has been changed dramatically from the original tale. In a sense, the tale has been broken apart and placed with other, unfamiliar elements. Sometimes several tales are combined to produce a work like *Into the Woods,* a Broadway musical by Stephen Sondheim.

Frame Tale. An overall tale that holds many narrative within it. Boccaccio's *Decameron* is an example of a frame tale. The overall story tells of a group of young aristocrats who have gone to the country to escape the plague in the city. While away, they each tell a set of stories. The group of young aristocrats serve as the frame for the stories within.

Function. The purpose or role that an item of folklore plays in a culture or in the life of the members of a culture.

Genre. A term used tentatively by folklorists, genre refers to categories such as form, content, style, and function.

Ghost Story. A narrative that contains supernatural elements usually designed to frighten or unsettle the listener.

Griot. An epic bard who tells traditional stories in West Africa. This role is usually a hereditary responsibility.

Hero Tale. Narratives that follow the pattern of the hero including: the call, the departure, the mentor, the adventure, hero deeds and dragon slayers, the road of trials, monster combat, the return, and the final victory.

Historical Literature. Nonfictional literature that conveys the historical and physical setting, characters, and culture of a frame of time.

Household Tale. The Märchen of Jacob and Wilhelm Grimm were originally called household tales because they were represented to be tales told by caregivers of children.

Humorous Anecdote. A short oral narrative that conveys something the teller finds funny.

Jack Tale. A fantastic adventure tale most associated with the rural South and Appalachia (but not limited to those regions) in which an adolescent male explores adult behavior by proving his prowess and talent. Jack is usually a trickster or fool in these tales, and he often either gets lucky or receives help from others. Typical stories may have foolish Jack trying to retrieve a reflected moon from a pond (with help), or a clever Jack outwitting devils. These narratives are favorites with many storytellers.

Joke. A humorous prose narrative that has an unexpected or surprise ending.

Journalism. Journalists gather, write, edit, verify, and publish or spread news by several media. Newspapers, magazines, radio, and television are venues for journalists. Some contemporary journalism is becoming more creative and includes creative nonfiction by literary and folkloric allusions and references.

Just So Story. The *Just So Stories,* originally published by Rudyard Kipling in 1902, are etiology tales of origins. Typical titles in the series are "How the Whale Got His Throat," "The Beginning of the Armadillos," and "How the Alphabet Was Made."

Kamishibai. These are Japanese story cards. The cards combine visual learning with oral transmission to convey folk stories. The practice is thousands of years old and is found all over the world from Japan to Indonesia, to India, the Near East, and throughout Europe.

Legend. Legends are stories that are exchanged about events in the recent past that are thought to be true. The main figures in legends are usually human, but legends can involve supernatural beings like ghosts, saints, and other mystical figures.

Leshii. Supernatural spirits who dwell in the deepest parts of the forest in Eastern Europe. They are said to be tricksters and shape-changers, with cloven hooves, horns, and thrashing tails. They confuse and sometimes kidnap travelers. There are many stories about them, and once when many squirrels were seen to be moving towards western Europe, the lore arose that the *leshii* on the European side had won them from the Siberians in a card game!

Limerick. A nonsense poem with five lines, usually rhyming AABBA. The form was popularized by Edward Lear (1812–88).

Literary Fairy Tale. An oral tale that has been composed into a literary form. Jacob and Wilhelm Grimm, Charles Perrault, and Giambattista Basile were among many who took spoken or oral tales and wrote them into literary fairy tales.

Magic. The use of spells, charms, or rituals in the pretended use of having power over natural or supernatural elements, events, or human behavior.

Märchen or *Conte Fabulaire*. A story or tale, particularly a folktale or fairy tale.

Material Folklore. Things people make. Examples: quilts, rugs, pottery, carvings, recipes, and other items people make with their hands.

Memorate. A narrative usually told by the person who experienced it about an encounter with the supernatural.

Metaphor. A metaphor is an analogous figure of speech in which one thing is described as though it were something else. The metaphor ascribes the qualities or characteristics of one thing to another. For instance, a storyteller might describe death as a long sleep, or the flight of a bird as freedom. An *extended metaphor* is one that is developed at length and involves many comparative points. A *mixed metaphor* is when two metaphors are inappropriately mixed together; for example, pebbles and satin are illogically mixed in: "Little sins are like pebbles in a shoe; seek the satin of repentance." A third type of metaphor is called a *dead metaphor*. This is one that has been overused so much that it has lost its metaphorical impact. Two examples are "the foot of the bed" and "toe the line."

Minstrel. A medieval class of entertainers who traveled from place to place to sing and recite stories with musical accompaniment.

Moral. Making distinctions between right and wrong conduct.

Motif. A motif is a very small component of a story. For instance, the pea would be the motif in the story of "The Princess and the Pea."

Mother Goose. The imaginary teller or narrator of a collection of tales (c.1697) by Charles Perrault.

Myth. A traditional story of unknown authorship serving usually to explain phenomena of nature such as the origin of the universe, humankind, or even customs and religious beliefs.

Narratology. Narratology studies the form, functioning, and nature of narrative and tries to determine authenticity and credibility (or narrative competence) of the tale. It looks at what tales have in common, and what is different about them.

Novella. A tale or short story, sometimes developed into a short novel. The tale, though short, is often complex.

Nursery Rhyme. Brief verses, usually anonymous, with clear rhythm and rhyme written for young children.

Old Wives' Tale. A superstitious belief or silly tale.

Parable. A story that teaches a lesson. It is often an allegory.

Participant Observation: A research strategy in folklore, anthropology, and ethnomusicology in which the fieldworker actively participates in the event (meal, musical performance, celebration, ritual, festival) and gains a broader understanding of what is happening and why.

Performance. A form of expressive culture rooted within culturally defined boundaries; a mode of communication that takes place between two or more people who share moments of the activity. It may be an oral communication, such as storytelling, poetic recitation, or drama, or it may be musical, or combinations of these and many other styles of communication. In folklore and story, it may be one teller communicating to an audience, or privately, it may be a simple person-to-person transmission of verbal lore.

Personal Narrative. A first-person narrative based on experiences in the life of the storyteller. In the telling, the cultural and personal values of the storyteller are often revealed.

Prose Narrative. A story, written or spoken, that does not have a regular, rhythmic pattern or metrical schemes.

Proverb. A saying that is usually passed along from person to person, or written, which expresses some recognized truth about life. Proverbs are often preserved in the oral tradition of a culture.

Pun. A play on words using words that are formed alike or sound alike but have different meanings. A pun is often humorous.

Revenant. In folklore, a revenant is a ghost.

Rhapsode. In ancient Greece, a rhapsode was a person who recited epic verses professionally.

Rhyme. Poetic language that involves the repetition of the line ending sounds.

Riddle. A verbal puzzle that poses a question or presents a problem. It requires the listener to decode the sentence or question to determine the answer.

Ritual, Rite. A traditional and symbolic form of behavior that is repeated over time. Rituals are often associated with religious myth, and because of the use of symbolism they are often complex and ambiguous.

Saga. A saga is an account of a heroic adventure, often applied to Icelandic and Nordic stories.

Sage. A wise person, often elderly and male, who is respected for intelligence and good judgment.

Saint's Legend. A saint's legend is written and gives an account of miracles to edify and strengthen peoples' belief in God. The Grimm brothers placed saints' legends at the end of their collection and called them children's legends.

Scatological. Folklore is the study of expressive culture. When recording and discussing anecdotes and traditions with many subjects, it is inevitable that humor is often derived from bodily functions. The trickster tales are often crude and graphic. Scatological tales or motifs often mention body excrement.

Schwank. A long narrative in which description of the characters or the unique situation carries the story rather than a punch line at the end.

Shaggy Dog Story. A long, drawn-out type of narrative that builds suspense and then concludes with a pun or play on words at the end.

Shape-Shifting. The ability to change from one form to another. Stories of the skin walkers in the Southwest United States describe evil human beings who can change into animals, usually coyotes or wolves, and then back into human form.

Simile. A simile is a figure of speech that compares two dissimilar things by using a key word such as *like* or *as*. The simile links the two items together by a common characteristic or resemblance in one aspect. For instance, "the skinny man seemed as tall as a flagpole," or "swiftly and gracefully, she ran like a deer."

Street Performer. A street performer often performs on a musical instrument, most commonly a guitar or violin, and he or she usually has something on the ground where money can be placed by passersby. Strangely enough, some musicians have been "discovered" in this way, and they have continued on to have successful, lucrative musical careers.

Story. An account that has a time sequence. A story usually has a beginning, middle, and end, as well as characters, tension, and resolution.

Storyteller. A teller of oral narrative. The narratives can be nontraditional, that is, not representative of the storyteller's culture or ethnicity. Or the stories can be traditional; that is, representative of the teller's heritage and transmitted over time by vernacular transfer from generation to generation.

Storytelling. Storytelling, whether it be traditional, nontraditional, anecdotal, gossip, rumor, didactic, or for entertainment, is something in which all cultures engage. It is an exchange of information from the teller to the hearer, and in many cases, this is the way cultural values and taboos are shared.

Superstition. A belief that a person holds even though they recognize that it is probably not valid. A superstition often arises from fear or ignorance and is based on information inconsistent with scientific law.

Survival. In a folkloric sense, an item that has literally survived in expressive culture over a long period of time. In survival theory, the concept is that contemporary folklore is derived from traditions that wind back into misty antiquity.

Symbol. A symbol is something that exists itself but stands for or represents something else. For instance, national flags are designs in cloth, but they are symbols of various countries. Some examples of common religious symbols are: the star of David, which represents Judaism; the cross, which represents Christianity; and the crescent, which represents Islam. A snake is sometimes used as a symbol for good or evil. Colors are used in various cultures to express symbolic meanings. These can vary greatly. For example, in the Western part of the world, black is the traditional symbol of mourning, whereas in the Eastern world, the traditional color symbol for mourning is white.

Synchronic. A point in time. A synchronic study considers or describes a culture at a particular point in time disregarding history and change. *See also* Diachronic.

Taboo. Off limits language, behavior, or even material items that are out of the bounds of propriety and good community decorum.

Talisman, Talismanic. An amulet, stone, or other trinket thought to bring good look or protect the bearer from evil. The object itself is thought to have magic power or to work as a charm.

Tall Tale. Usually humorous, a tall tale is an exaggerated lie told with a straight face. A tall tale is sometimes called a windy.

Theme. A theme is the central idea of poetry, fiction, or drama.

Trickster. A trickster is a person who lies, cheats, or otherwise deceives. The trickster plays both positive and negative roles in the narratives of society, and the trickster sometimes reveals truths to the audience through abstract and deceptive methods.

Trickster Tale. Trickster tales often feature animals that play tricks of deception. American folktales often depict the coyote or rabbit as trickster figures.

Type. A type is a recurring pattern of story or narrative elements. Versions of a particular tale type may be told in various versions or variants in several different cultures. For example, the story of Cinderella, that is the female rags-to-riches tale type, has been found in over 1,500 cultures to date. While no two of the stories are exactly alike, the plot structure or outline can be identified. Stories similar to the European Cinderella have been found in the storytelling traditions of cultures in Europe, Persia, China, Japan, the Caribbean, Cambodia, and more. The basic tale is a conceptual prototype, and thousands of tales have been collected and categorized in various tale-typing systems.

Urban Legend. Urban legends have developed in contemporary culture and seem to reflect the fears of society. The stories can range from stories of horror to stories of humor.

Variant, Version. A variant is a different version of a tale, myth, or literary passage. Oral telling and transmission of story and/or folklore inevitably creates individualized versions. When the story varies widely from the version most commonly known, it is called a variant. An example would be the Hebrew story of Noah and the flood. Throughout recorded history, there have been stories of world floods that differ greatly from the Hebrew narrative. Some of these variants parallel the Hebrew Bible story (*Gilgamesh*). Stories can be called variants when they bear little resemblance to one another beyond the similarity of basic motifs.

Vernacular Folklore. Vernacular, in this sense, refers to oral or verbal narratives.

Wonder Tale. Wonder tale is a synonym for fairy tale, magic tale, Märchen, or ordinary folktale. It is the kind of tale where fantasy comfortably blends with reality to create a believable story. In a wonder tale, a dirty girl can be transformed into a sparkling princess with glass slippers in the twinkling of an eye by a simple wave of a magic wand. Somehow, it seems believable when the reader is engaged with the story.

Bibliography

REFERENCE WORKS

Brown, Mary Ellen, and Bruce A. Rosenberg, eds. *Encyclopedia of Folklore and Literature*. Santa Barbara, CA: ABC-CLIO, 1998.

Brunvand, Jan Harold, ed. *American Folklore: An Encyclopedia*. New York: Garland, 1996.

Pellowski, Anne. *The World of Storytelling*. New York: R. R. Bowker, 1977.

TOOLS FOR TEACHERS

Adler, Bill, Jr. *Tell Me a Fairy Tale: A Parent's Guide to Telling Magical and Mythical Stories*. New York: Penguin, 1995.

Beach, Richard. *A Teacher's Introduction to Reader Response Theories*. Urbana, IL: National Council of Teachers of English, 1993.

Bosma, Bette. *Fairy Tales, Fables, Legends, and Myths: Using Folk Literature in Your Classroom*. New York: Teacher's College Press, 1992.

Bronner, Simon J. *American Children's Folklore*. Little Rock, AR: August House, 1988.

Goforth, Frances S., And Carolyn V. Spillman. *Using Folk Literature in the Classroom: Encouraging Children to Read and Write*. Phoenix, AZ: Oryx Press, 1994.

Narayan, Kirin. *Storytellers, Saints, and Scoundrels: Folk Narrative in Hindu Religious Teaching*. Philadelphia: University of Pennsylvania Press, 1989.

Norman, Renee. *House of Mirrors: Performing Autobiographically in Language/Education*. New York: Peter Lang, 2001.

Pugh, Sharon L., Jean Wolph Hicks, and Marcia Davis. *Metaphorical Ways of Knowing: The Imaginative Nature of Thought and Expression*. Urbana, IL: National Council of Teachers of English, 1997.

Roe, Betty D., Suellen Alfred, and Sandy Smith. *Teaching through Stories: Yours, Mine, and Theirs.* Norwood, MA: Christopher-Gordon, 1998.

Rosenblatt, Louise. *Making Meaning with Texts: Selected Essays.* Portsmouth, NH: Heinemann, 2005.

Simons, Elizabeth Radin. *Student Worlds Student Words: Teaching Writing through Folklore.* Portsmouth, NH: Boynton/Cook Heinemann, 1990.

Sobol, Joseph Daniel. *The House between Earth and Sky: Harvesting New American Folktales.* Portsmouth, NH: Teacher Ideas Press, 2005.

MULTINATIONAL COLLECTIONS

Faces: The Magazine about People. Published by Cobblestone Publishing, this magazine covers a variety of traditional and folkloric customs. See http://www.cobblestonepub.com for further information.

Jackson, Ellen. *Here Come the Brides.* Walker and Company, 1998. This is a text about various brides and bridal lore and customs around the world. For instance, in Greece, a bride throws a ripe pomegranate at a door smeared with honey. If the seeds stick to the door, people believe that the marriage will be happy and blessed with many children. Folk practices included in the book range from dying the hands with henna and wearing red on the wedding day to a bridal custom of adorning the face with white dots.

NONTRADITIONAL COLLECTIONS

Finnegan, Ruth. *Oral Traditions and the Verbal Arts: A Guide to Research Practices.* New York: Routledge, 1992.

Foley, John Miles. *How to Read an Oral Poem.* Urbana: University of Chicago, 2002.

Foley, John Miles. *Teaching Oral Traditions.* New York: Modern Language Association, 1998.

BOOKS ABOUT FOLKLORE

Brunvand, Jan Harold. *The Study of American Folklore: An Introduction.* New York: W. W. Norton, 1998.

Georges, Robert A., and Michael Owen Jones. *Folkloristics: An Introduction.* Bloomington: Indiana University Press, 1995.

Lindahl, Carl, John McNamara, and John Lindow. eds. *Medieval Folklore: A Guide to Myths, Legends, Tales, Beliefs, and Customs.* New York: Oxford University Press, 2002.

BOOKS ABOUT FOLK AND FAIRY TALES

Ashliman, D. L. *Folk and Fairy Tales: A Handbook.* Westport, Connecticut: Greenwood Press, 2004.

de Vos, Gail, and Anna E. Altmann. *New Tales for Old: Folktales as Literary Fictions for Young Adults.* Englewood, CO: Libraries Unlimited, 1999.

Hallett, Martin, and Barbara Karasek, eds. *Folk and Fairy Tales.* 3d ed. New York: Broadview Press, 2002.

Harries, Elizabeth Wanning. *Twice upon a Time: Women Writers and the History of the Fairy Tale.* Princeton, NJ: Princeton University Press, 2001.

Sierra, Judy. *Silly and Sillier: Read-Aloud Tales from around the World.* Alfred Knopf, 2002.

Tatar, Maria. *The Hard Facts of the Grimms' Fairy Tales.* Princeton: Princeton University Press, 2003.

Zipes, Jack David. *Sticks and Stones: The Troublesome Success of Children's Literature from Slovenly Peter to Harry Potter.* New York: Routledge, 2001.

Zipes, Jack David, ed. *The Great Fairy Tale Tradition: From Straparola and Basile to the Brothers Grimm.* New York: W. W. Norton, 2001.

BOOKS ABOUT THE TRICKSTER FIGURE

Hyde, Lewis. *Trickster Makes This World: Mischief, Myth, and Art.* New York: North Point Press, 1998.

Hynes, William J., and William G. Doty, eds. *Mythical Trickster Figures: Contours, Contexts, and Criticisms.* Tuscaloosa: University of Alabama Press, 1997.

Radin, Paul. *The Trickster: A Study in American Indian Mythology.* New York: Schocken Books, 1972.

BOOKS ABOUT REGIONAL FOLKLORE

Anderson, Janet Alm. *Bounty: A Harvest of Food Lore and Country Memories from Utah's Past.* Boulder, CO: Pruett Publishing, 1990.

Barden, Thomas, ed. *Virginia Folk Legends.* Charlottesville: University Press of Virginia, 1991.

Brasch, Walter M. *Brer Rabbit, Uncle Remus, and the "Cornfield Journalist."* Macon, GA: Mercer University Press, 2000.

Bringhurst, Robert. *A Story as Sharp as a Knife: The Classical Haida Mythtellers and Their World.* Lincoln: University of Nebraska Press, 1999.

Butler, Anne M., and Ona Siporin. *Uncommon Common Women: Ordinary Lives of the West.* Logan: Utah State University Press, 1996.

Hufford, Mary, Marjorie Hunt, and Steven J. Zeitlin. *The Grand Generation: Memory, Mastery, and Legacy.* Washington, D.C., Smithsonian Traveling Exhibition Service. Seattle: University of Washington Press, 1987.

Saxon, Lyle, Edward Dreyer, and Robert Tallant. *Gumbo Ya-Ya: A Collection of Louisiana Folk Tales.* Gretna, Louisiana: Pelican Publishing, 1998.

Toelken, Barre. *The Anguish of Snails: Native American Folklore in the West.* Logan: Utah State University Press, 2003.

Zeitlan, Steve, et. al. *A Celebration of American Family Folklore.* New York: Pantheon Books, 1982.

BOOKS ABOUT GENDER ISSUES AND FOLKLORE

Bell, Elizabeth, Lynda Haas, and Laura Sells. *From Mouse to Mermaid: The Politics of Film, Gender, and Culture.* Bloomington: Indiana University Press, 1995.
Jordan, Rosan A., and Susan J. Kalčik, eds. *Women's Folklore, Women's Culture.* Pennsylvania: University of Pennsylvania Press, 1985.
Warner, Marina. *From the Beast to the Blond: On Fairy Tales and Their Tellers.* New York: Farrar, Straus and Giroux, 1996.

BOOKS ABOUT STORY AND STORYTELLING

Bauman, Richard. *Story, Performance, and Event: Contextual Studies of Oral Narrative.* Cambridge: Press Syndicate of the University of Cambridge, 1986.
Lipman, Doug. *Improving Your Storytelling: Beyond the Basics for All Who Tell Stories in Work or Play.* Little Rock, AR: August House, 1999.
Mooney, Bill and David Holt, eds. *The Storyteller's Guide: Storytellers Share Advice for the Classroom, Boardroom, Showroom Podium, Pulpit, and Center Stage.* Little Rock, AR: August House, 1996.
Stotter, Ruth. *The Golden Axe and Other Folktales of Compassion and Greed.* Oakland, CA: Stotter Press, 1998.

JOURNALS

Marvels and Tales
Parabola
Children's Folklore Review
The Lion and the Unicorn

Web Resources

INTRODUCTION

In the following presentation book titles are given in *italic type* and Web site names in **bold type.**

The Internet is a valuable center for folklore and story information, and the material on the net has improved with time. Even so, some information is not credible and some, because of copyright infringements, is not even legal. New sites and materials are added daily, and old sites often change their addresses or disappear altogether without a forwarding address. This makes an up-to-date list of working sites a dynamic process. Using the search engines as a supplement, rather than a primary research, eliminates some disappointment and frustration that comes with researching on the ever-mercurial Internet.

SEARCH ENGINES

The most effective search engine I have found is **Metacrawler** (http://www.metacrawler.com). Nearly any noun, topic, or combination of words typed into the window will result in a useful list of sites. **Metacrawler** is forgiving in that it will often search for the topic even if the initial request is slightly misspelled. Listed below are several other search engines that have proven dependable and are easily accessible:

Google (http://www.google.com)
All the Web (http://alltheweb.com)
Alta Vista (http://altavista.org)

DMOZ (http://dmoz.org)
Excite (http://www.excite.com).
Lycos (http://www.lycos.com)
Teoma (http://www.teoma.com)
Webcrawler (http://www.webcrawler.com)
WiseNut (http://www.wisenut.com)
Yahoo! (http://www.yahoo.com)

ENCYCLOPEDIAS AND GENERAL REFERENCE WORKS

General encyclopedias and reference works are excellent resources for finding helpful historical and contextual facts for storytelling. Basic information about authors, collectors, movements, and genres is also given, and story plots and short versions of popular narratives are often included.
The Columbia Encyclopedia (online):

- **Bartleby.com** (http://www.bartleby.com)

- **Encyclopedia.com** (http://www.encyclopedia.com)

- **Infoplease.com** (http://www.infoplease.com)

Microsoft's *Encarta* encyclopedia: (http://encarta.msn.com)
Encyclopedia Britannica of 1911 (online): (http://75.1911encyclopedia.org)
Dictionary of the History of Ideas (1973–74): (http://etext.lib.virginia.edu/DicHist/dict.html)

RESEARCH LIBRARIES

The following list of large European and North American libraries provides online catalogs for bibliographic information about published myth, legend, and folktale books. These listings provide sufficient information to enable the user to find or order (through outside circulation) the listed texts in a local public or university library.

COPAC (British Library and university libraries in the United Kingdom and Ireland): (http://copac.ac.uk/copac/)
Gabriel (The World Wide Web service of Europe's national libraries): (http//: www.kb.nl/gabriel/)
Library of Congress (U.S.): (http://www/loc.gov/)
Folklore Sourcebook (U.S.): (http://www.loc.gov/folklife/source/sourcebk.html)
Libweb (Internet resources from libraries in more than 115 countries): (http:// sunsite.berkeley.edu/Libweb/)

Melvyl (University of California Libraries): (http://melvyl.cdlib.org/)
World eBook Library (University of Pennsylvania): (http://onlinebooks.library.
upenn.edu/titles.html)

ELECTRONIC TEXT INDEXES

Many myths, legends, fables, and folktales can be found on the Internet as
electronic texts. Some are free, and some are available for a fee.

Online Books (University of Pennsylvania): (http://digital.library.upenn.edu/
books/)
Digital Book Index (University of Pennsylvania and commercial titles): (http://dig-
italbookindex.com/)

DIRECTORIES OF ELECTRONIC TEXT
SITES (ALL SUBJECTS)

DMOZ (directory of electronic text archives): (http://dmoz.org/Arts/Literature/
Electronic_Text_Archives/)
Google (directory of electronic text archives): (http://directory.google.com/Top/
Arts/Literature/Electronic_Text_Archives)
Yahoo! (directory of electronic literature (http://dir.yahoo.com/Arts/Humanities/
Literature/Electronic_Literature/)

DIRECTORIES OF MYTH, LEGEND, FAIRY
TALE, AND FOLKTALE SITES

Listed below are Web sites that have countless links to myths, legends,
fairy tales and folktales from around the world.

Folklore, Myth, and Legend: (http://acs.ucalgary.ca/~dkbrown/storfolk.html)
Myths and Legends—frames: (http://home.comcast.net/~chris.s/myth.html)
Regional Folklore and Mythology: (http://www.pibburns.com/mythregi-htm)
American Folklore: (http://www.americanfolklore.net/)
Myth, Legend, Folklore, Ghosts: (http://www.teacheroz.com/myth-legend.htm)
Canadian Folklore: Myths, Legends, Folktales, Fairytales: (http://www.american-
folklore.net/canada.html)
Appalachian Folktales in Children's Literature and Collections: (http://www.
ferrum.edu/applit/bibs/FolkBib.htm)
The Serene Dragon: Sources of the Myths, Tales, Legends, and Other Stories:
(http: www.theserenedragon.net/sources.html)

FOLKLORE, STORY, AND EDUCATION

American Folklore Society Folklore and Education Section Newsletter. (http://www.afsnet.org/sections/education/Spring2005)

The 2005 CARTS Culture Catalogue furnishes authentic teaching resources in folk arts, folklore, and oral history—from folktales to documenting neighborhoods, family history, to math games. (http://www.carts.org)

Florida Folklife Collection Online. Twenty years of records from Florida's Folklife Program. The site includes information, images, and links. There are over 50,000 images and 5,000 audio recordings. (http://www.floridamemory.com/Collections/folklife/index.cfm)

American Folklife Center's Veteran's History Project website. (http://www.loc.gov.folklife/vets/youth-resources.html). Contact Peter Bartis: phone, 202-707-4919: e-mail, peba@loc.gov.

Louisiana Voices. Folklore lessons with background, activities, and interviewing strategies. (http://www.louisianavoices.org)

Masters of Ceremony. Master folk artists provide a window into the way several ethnic groups mark the rites of passage: birth, coming of age, marriage, and death. (http://www.ohw.org/exhibitions/moc)

"Preserve the Stories of Your Family and Community. The Smithsonian Folklife and Oral History Interviewing Guide. Available to download. (http://www.folklife.si.edu./explore/resources). Contact Marjorie Hunt: phone, 202-275-2025; e-mail, marjorie@folklife.si.edu.

Rites of Passage in America. This online Balch Institute for Ethnic Studies exhibit includes essays and images. (http://www2.hsp.org/exhibits/Balch%20exhibits/rites/lifecycle.html)

FOLKLORE AND MUSIC

Richard Burgess, at the Smithsonian/Folkways, has informed the public that "The Smithsonian Center for Folklife and Cultural Heritage announces the launch of our highly anticipated web site, **Smithsonian Global Sound.** It offers downloads of music and sound from around the world. The site has a wealth of educational content and downloads are accompanied by extensive liner notes. Our goal is to encourage local musicians and traditions around the planet through international recognition, the payment of royalties, and support for regional archives. Users can browse by genre, instrument, geographical location, and cultural group and enjoy Artist Features and Radio Global Sound. Subscriptions are available for educational institutions. We welcome suggestions on how to improve our site to meet the needs of educators, students, and fans of great music." (http://www.smithsonianglobalsound.org)

Smithsonian Folkways Recordings offers nearly 300 commercial recordings and over 3,000 made-to-order archival titles of American folk music, traditional world music, children's music and spoken word—all with original liner notes. The web site offers 30-second sound clips of the 40,000 tracks in the archive. (http://www.folkways.si.edu)

GENERAL STORYTELLER'S SITES

Jonesborough Storytelling Guild: (http://www.storytellersguild.org/main.htm)
Storypage: Links to Storytelling Websites: (http://www.ac.wwu.edu/~rvos/Storytelling/storytellinglinks.htm)
Story-Telling.com: (http://www.story-telling.com/References/WebSites.htm)
Navigating the Storytelling Ring: (http://www.storydynamica.com/resources/storyring.html)
Center for Digital Storytelling: (http://www.storycenter.org/index1.html)
Storytelling Resources: (http://user.icx.net/~richmond/smsa/recourselist.html)
Tim Sheppard's Storytelling Resources for Storytellers: Stories: (http://timsheppard.co.uk/story/storylinks.html)

ORGANIZATIONS AND JOURNALS

American Folklore Society: (http://afsnet.org/)
Children's Literature Association: (http://ebbs.english.vt.edu/chla/)
Folklinks: (http://www.pitt.edu/~dash/folklinks.html)
Storytelling: (http://www.eldrbarry.net/roos/art.html)
Storytelling, Self, Society: An Interdisciplinary Journal of Storytelling Studies: (http://courses.unt.edu/efiga/SSS/ContentsNews.htm)
Marvels and Tales: (http://www.langlab.wayne.edu/MarvelsHome/Marvels_Tales.html)
The Lion and the Unicorn: (http://www.press.jhu.edu/journals/)

Index

About the Author

JACQUELINE S. THURSBY is Associate Professor of English at Brigham Young University, where she specializes in folklore studies. Her previous books include *Mother's Table, Father's Chair: Cultural Narratives of Basque American Women* (1999).